Never Repress
LAUGHTER

Stories to Bring Smiles, Memories, and Gratitude

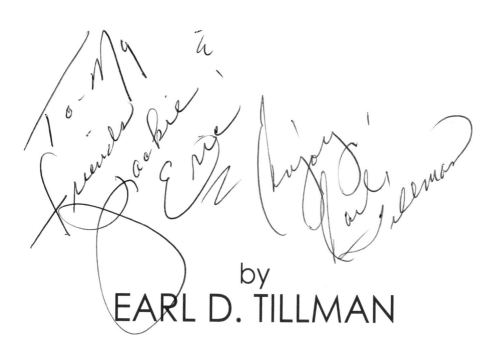

by
EARL D. TILLMAN

© 2018

Published in the United States by Nurturing Faith Inc., Macon GA,

www.nurturingfaith.net.

Library of Congress Cataloging-in-Publication Data is available.

ISBN 978-1-63528-052-4

In memory of
My twin brother, Ed Tillman
My sister, Josephine (Jo) Tillman Winters
My son, Gary Tillman
and
My sweet granddaughter, Hannah Gail Tillman

In honor of
My wife, Carolyn Bagwell Tillman
My daughter, Tamara Tillman Smathers
My son-in-law Jeff Smathers
My daughter-in-law, Denise Dooley Tillman Rowland
My granddaughters, Rachel Tillman Peaden and Bonnie Grace Tillman
and
My great-granddaughters, Ella and Emma Peaden
They all have the gift of laughter.

About the Author

Earl Tillman is a popular speaker and community leader in Rome, Georgia, where he lives with his wife, Carolyn. They are longtime, active members of the First Baptist Church there.

Earl grew up on a farm in South Georgia but has long made Northwest Georgia his home. He has had a distinguished career in the insurance business and other enterprises. Additionally, he served as assistant to the president at Berry College—on the beautiful, sprawling mountain campus where he attended high school. His deep and continuing love of aviation as a pilot and flight instructor recently led to the naming of "Earl Tillman Drive" at the Richard B. Russell Airport in Floyd County, Georgia.

Earl's good life—filled with faith, family, fun, and flying—flows through the pages of this book. He is a storyteller and encourager. Relax, read, think, smile, and laugh along.

Storytelling in the rural South has long been an art form. Prior to radio and television, it was a major form of communication and entertainment.

The stories in this collection come from actual experiences. However, as time passed, some of the facts merged with a bit of fiction. No storyteller would ever let the whole truth get in the way of a good story. The best stories get passed along from person to person and generation to generation. May this book add to the long tradition of passing along delightful stories and a dose of joy.

Over many years Earl has had the opportunity to speak to various audiences from the Bahamas to San Juan to China and all across the United States. Should you wish to invite him to speak to your company convention, civic club, chamber of commerce meeting, church banquet, or another setting, please let him hear from you at (706) 346-7557 or (706) 235-9840.

❖

Contents

Introduction

Storytelling in the rural South has long been an art form. Prior to radio and television, it was a major form of communication and entertainment.

The stories in this collection come from actual experiences. However, as time passed, some of the facts merged with a bit of fiction. No storyteller would ever let the whole truth get in the way of a good story. The best stories get passed along from person to person and generation to generation. Parents enjoyed telling of their childhood years, and the stories got even better as the grandparents and great-grandparents expanded on the truths and added some of their own.

Thanks to friend and fellow author Merrill Davies for her help; to Dr. Ross West and my wife, Carolyn, for spelling words for me; to my granddaughter for her helpful communication skills; and to Janice Hudson-Huff for making the computer look simple.

This book will continue in part as an autobiography. Hopefully you will be able to think of your own family—the good days and years you had, the laughter and the sad times you have shared.

As in most families, when sharing a story or event, I will digress now and then. It is like when you are talking with family or friends and you have a flashback to another happy or sad time.

Some of these stories are excerpts from a speech I gave. Enjoy them as if you were there.

Ugly Survey

One icebreaker I use when speaking to a group: It seems that every organization or company is doing a study or running a survey. Recently, I saw a survey that I don't believe holds true here tonight. The survey indicated that one person out of every three in this country is ugly.

Let's test this survey tonight. Will everyone please look at the person on your right? Now look to the one on your left. If they look okay, then apparently you're it!

Forks, Spoons, and Knives

Another icebreaker: Larry (the person in charge of the event) and I were talking about how important this event would be. I told him with such an important group I would not do anything that would embarrass him or his wife, Moni.

He said there were several persons here to watch as good examples. They are national and international travelers. They know which fork, spoon, and knife to pick up first. You could watch Wayne Holsonback, Dan Oswald, Ken Magnuson, Henry Duke, or Dan Hope, he said.

"Why don't you watch our longtime friend Wayne Holsonback?" he asked. I knew Larry had suggested the right person when Wayne tipped his little finger and drank his tea. He seemed to know exactly how to pick up his fork, spoon, and knife. I guess I did everything just like Wayne.

But I don't feel I should do everything Wayne did. So I'm just going to put these back on the table (pulling several forks, spoons, and knives from coat pocket and placing them on table). How is that for an ice breaker for your next presentation?

My Friends at the High Rise

I taught a Sunday school class for several years at the local high rise. Wonderful people live there. When you get ready to retire and you do not have a special place to live, let me invite you to come to the high rise in our town.

The ratio of women to men at the high rise is around 10:1. There was one ol' boy who was able to get himself a date with Louise. Louise wanted it to be a good date, so she went to the drugstore on the corner and bought a big bag of caramel candy. She put the candy on the seat between them, and they drove to the drive-in movie theater.

They parked, the lights went out, and the movie came on. Soon, the man bent down and started feeling around in the floorboard of the car. Louise asked him, "What are you looking for?"

The man said, "I'm looking for my candy."

She said, "Silly, we have a big bag in the seat between us."

In a nearly frustrated voice he said, "I know, but this piece has my teeth in it."

When they got back to the high rise, the ladies were waiting for a report.

"How did it go?" they all asked.

Louise said, "I had to slap the old goat three times."

"Did he get fresh?" they asked.

"No, I thought he died."

Another Trip to the High Rise

One Saturday during check-in at the high rise, I was visiting my Sunday school class members and noticed a man checking in at the front desk. As he completed some forms, one of the ladies stood and watched him.

She looked and looked and looked at him. He turned and said, "Lady, why do you keep looking at me?"

She said, "You look just like my third husband."

He replied, "My, my, how many times have you been married?"

She answered, "Twice."

Now I will slow down if some of you are having trouble keeping up.

Misprints in Church Bulletins

If you think you have a problem, consider your minister, pastor, or priest. He or she has been so busy during the week conducting funerals, visiting the sick, performing weddings, and preparing for Sunday's message that they may not have had time to proofread the bulletin before Sunday's services.

Here are some examples of unintended meanings passed along through the years:

• This afternoon there will be a baptism in the south and north ends of the church. Children will be baptized on both ends.

• Tuesday at 4 p.m. there will be an ice cream social. All ladies giving milk please come early.

• Wednesday the Ladies Literary Society will meet. Mrs. Johnson will sing "Put Me in My Little Bed," accompanied by the pastor.

• Thursday at 5 p.m. there will be a meeting of the Little Mothers Club. All wishing to become Little Mothers will meet with the minister in his study.

• This being Easter Sunday, we will ask Mrs. Johnson to come forward and lay an egg on the altar.

• The service will close with "Little Drops of Water." One of the ladies will start quietly, and the rest will join in.

• If you have children and do not know it, the nursery is on the second floor.

• This morning a special collection will be taken to defray the expenses on the new carpet. All wishing to do something on the carpet please come forward and get a little piece of paper.

A Great Listener

Charlie and Agnes had been married for more than fifty years. Their great desire was to go for an airplane ride, so they drove to the local airport.

They saw a big sign that read, "Airplane Rides $25." The price caused a great discussion between them. The pilot came over and told them if they would be quiet, listen, and not say anything during the ride, it would not cost the full $25, but if they talked, it would cost the total amount.

Charlie turned and said, "Mama, let's go!" The pilot put them in the back seat of the open cockpit aircraft and taxied to the runway.

The pilot made a good preflight check, rolled onto the runway, and applied full power. The plane lifted off the ground. With a quick climb to 2,000 feet, the pilot rolled the plane, then climbed to 3,000 feet.

He then rolled into a steep turn to the right, then to the left. After a couple stalls, they came back to the airport. The pilot made a beautiful landing, and as he taxied, he looked over his shoulder and said, "Sir, you were a good listener and did not say anything. It will not cost you $25."

The man said, "Yes, sir, but I would have liked to have said something the first time you rolled the plane and Agnes fell out."

Getting Better

No matter where we are in our career, business, profession, trade, marriage, or social life, we can get better.

My friend Al has become an excellent pilot. He has a private pilot's license, and I had the honor of working with him to get his instrument rating. However, he was not always as good as he is now.

When we teach people to fly, one of the great lessons is to "go around" if things are not going as planned. Al came around for the landing, bounced a couple times, and then applied full power and flew the traffic pattern for another landing. It did not look good.

After a third time the people in the terminal building said, "To the pilot in the Cessna, to the pilot in the Cessna, could we give you some help?"

Al picked up the mic and said, "There is no pilot up here. I'm up here by myself."

It's wonderful to be part of a church, company, or organization where we are not alone. Al has become a pro at what he does. So it's not where you were but what you can become.

Pulpwood Cutter in the Air Force

It is common knowledge in Northwest Georgia that Armuchee and Coosa are the places to live in Floyd County. Both have great respect for each other and seem to like each other until the football or basketball season heats up.

Knowing the rules helps. Number one: Get in the game.

One ol' boy from Armuchee and one from Coosa got real patriotic one Saturday evening after a few hours of a high-level social. Maybe the selection of their favorite Saturday night drink got the best of their decision-making.

"Let's join the Air Force and request an assignment in Baghdad," one suggested. The other agreed.

Monday, they arrived at the recruiting office. The young man from Armuchee went first to see the recruiter.

The Air Force recruiter asked, "What do you do?"

"Pile it," he responded.

"Great! We need a pilot. Sign here."

The young man from Coosa entered, and the recruiter asked, "What do you do?"

He responded, "I cut pulpwood."

"Well, we don't need any pulpwood cutters," said the recruiter.

"But you took my friend," said the man from Coosa.

"But he is a pilot," said the recruiter.

"Yes," said the Coosa man, "but he can't *pile it* if I don't cut it."

Sheep Bell

Our daughter, Tamara, worked in the Middle East for several years. We were able to visit with her in Jordan, Israel, and Egypt. There have been many changes in these areas since the days of Jesus, but the countryside is much like it was 2,000 years ago. I found the sheep bell and wrote the following about sheep and the sheep bell. I hope you find it interesting:

The sheep bell in the twenty-first century is much like the bell shepherds used over 2,000 years ago. The Bible refers to sheep more than 500 times, and the domestication of sheep dates back to 900 BC. Sheep provided food, wool for clothes, hide for tents, and horns for musical instruments.

The Bible provides several references to the skill of the shepherd, who knew each of his sheep by name and whose voice his sheep recognized (John 10:3–4). Jesus refers to sheep in several parables, and the Gospel of John portrays Jesus as a protecting shepherd, willing to give his life for his sheep.

A special gift I have given comes from a hardware store in Madaba, Jordan, where many shepherds still shop today. In your Bible, Madaba may be spelled M-a-d-e-b-a or M-e-d-e-b-a. Madaba is six miles from Mount Nebo, where Moses was allowed to view the promised land and near where the Jordan River flows into the Dead Sea.

On my visits to the Middle East, I often thought of my friends who teach Sunday school, sing in the choir, usher, sweep the floors, and cook church suppers and our pastors, ministers, and preachers who lead and shepherd their flock week after week. Hopefully this gift is a reminder of the Good Shepherd.

A few days ago, I was surfing the TV channels and saw a "Billy Graham Classic." It looked like an early 1950s revival at a big ballfield in California. He looked young and could really preach.

Much of the message was about sheep and the Good Shepherd. It made me proud that I had written about the sheep bell and the history of sheep and reminded us of the Good Shepherd.

Ol' Kicker the Frog

There is another gift I like to give: a frog. I'm not sure if Ol' Kicker is male or female.

Some of you know I was reared, raised, or jerked up on a small South Georgia farm. Every morning of my young life, my twin brother, Ed, and I milked our family cow, Betsy. I would hold the pot with my left hand and milk with my right. Ed would milk with both hands. It didn't take very long; Betsy was not a very good giver.

A few years back, I was speaking at an insurance convention in Port Jefferson, New York, and telling about Ol' Kicker. I asked for a show of hands of those who had milked a cow. One lady yelled, "We don't milk at Kroger!"

Those of you who have done some milking know that most of the time a couple frogs will be hopping around in the cow lot. This time, two frogs jumped in a bucket of milk. That is a pail for you teachers.

They started kicking just as hard as they could. The frogs, not the teachers. One frog said to the other, "We are not going to get out."

So he went goggle, goggle to the bottom, and I guess you know what happened. He drowned.

But the other frog just kept on kicking. Soon, he felt something firm and hard under his feet. Do you know what it was? Yes, it was a big lump of butter. The frog jumped on the butter, out of the bucket.

I was telling this story at Coosa High School, and there must have been about 800 students present. There was a young girl near the front. Nothing I said seemed to captivate her interest, until I started talking about Ol' Kicker.

Then I asked the question, "Do you know what the frog jumped on?"

The girl jumped out of her seat and said, "Yes, sir, I know! He jumped up on the other old dead frog."

I thought to myself, "My, my, that may be the best message of the story." So many people feel they climb the ladder of success by stepping on other people. We have seen lots of that in the news lately: business people taking advantage of elderly people by stealing their life savings; sports people not telling the truth, projecting a sorry image to our young people who look up to them. Hopefully, we know the best way to climb the ladder of success is to set the best example possible and help others in need.

I am reminded of the second-grade teacher who tried to explain the importance of being kind to others and sharing with others. The teacher said, "We were put on earth to help others."

A little girl asked, "Why were 'others' put here?"

Miracle Gem

When I am on the speaking circuit, I like to leave gifts at the attendees' plates and reference them in my speech. I told one audience, "I have left a special gem for you at your plate. I brought it to you from Edinburgh, Scotland. I tell you that just to brag."

Then I continue to unravel the story: Until I was seventeen years old, I had never been more than thirty miles from our small, rural South Georgia community. We used to go to nearby Blackshear, Waycross, and Alma on Saturday and brag during the week about what we had seen. Now, some of you probably go from Rome to Chattanooga or Atlanta and *not* tell anyone what you saw.

Take the gem, and carry it in your pocket. Rub it on the round side, and let it remind you of all the good things you want to do for your church, community, people you meet, family, and friends.

As you rub the round side of the miracle gem and do the things you have been taught to do at home and work, it will bring a miracle in your life. Turn the gem and rub the flat side, and it will help you in your love life.

Here is an extra gem for Larry. He asked for one that is flat on both sides.

Royal Air Force Museum

Several years ago we were in London, England, and visited the nearby Royal Air Force Museum. It was great to see the history of the Royal Air Force. Much has been written about the Royal Navy but not quite so much about the Royal Air Force.

Some of Winston Churchill's speeches were on display. A world leader prior to and during World War II, he inspired the British Empire to achieve seemingly impossible goals.

Some of Churchill's writings were serious, and some had a degree of humor. I will paraphrase much of this in honor of my ninth-grade English teacher, Mrs. Martha Harrison (it took me two years to get out of that class):

One evening, Mr. Churchill was at a party, and Lady Aster was there. Lady Aster loved royalty and liked to do what she perceived as proper. Mr. Churchill was enjoying his drinks and smoking a big cigar. Lady Aster had about all she could take.

"Mr. Churchill," she said, "you are obnoxious and nearly drunk."

"Yes, my lady, and you are ugly, and tomorrow I will be sober!"

At another meeting a female member of parliament said, "Mr. Churchill, if I were married to you, I would put arsenic in your tea."

He responded, "Yes, my lady, and if I were married to you, I would drink it."

On a serious note Mr. Churchill was paying tribute to the royal Air Force—the pilots and crews who flew round-the-clock missions knocking out German bombers as they bombed London and all of England. He noted, "Never has so much been done for so many, by so few."

Hopefully, when the history books are written, they will say about us as individuals and all of us collectively, "Never has so much been done for so many, by so few."

Camping Trip

It is a special gift to be able to laugh. Most adults will have a hearty laugh 30 times a day. Children will have a big laugh 300 times a day.

My mother, Bertie Mae, retired from the Slash Pine Community Action in Blackshear, Georgia. My dad, Edgar ("Ed" to his friends and kin), retired from the Merchant Marines. They bought an Eldorado camper, which was a Dodge truck with a sleeper over the truck cab, with a kitchen sink, table, couch, and an inside toilet, I believe. Like most campers, they did most of their cooking and talking outside. The vehicle even had a hitch so they could pull a jon boat on short trips.

My parents joined a camping club and traveled to Florida, Georgia, Tennessee, Kentucky, and Indiana. Mostly they took camping trips near home to places like Laura S. Walker Park near Waycross or on the St. Mary River, which divides Georgia and Florida.

When Tamara was about eight years old, her granddad told her of this camping event. I am not sure if he could say Tamara, because he just called her "Camery."

Tamara was sitting in the middle of the bed with her legs crossed under her waiting for him to tell her a story. He pulled his chair next to the bed and said, "Camery, this is our last camping trip. You see, I told your Granny Bertie to put all the groceries in a box and fill up all the jugs with fresh water so I could put them in the camper.

"Camery, we were going on a camping trip on the St. Mary River. We got up early to meet some of our camping friends, and if we got there early, we could get a good camping site near the river and close to the showers and restrooms. You see, Camery, when you are our age, you don't want to park too far from the restrooms. Do you understand that, Camery?"

Camery replied, "Yes, sir, at my age me neither."

He continued, "When we got about halfway to the St. Mary's River, I got pretty tired. I said to your Granny Bertie, 'Can you drive this rig?'"

She said, "I sure can."

"Now, Bertie Mae, remember President Carter set the speed limit at fifty-five miles per hour. I'll pull over to the side of the road; you can slide over to the driver's side. You sure you can drive this rig?"

She assured him she could.

"I said, 'Give me a few minutes to go to the back, open the door, pull off my shoes and pants, and get in the bed.' You know what she did, Camery? About the time I got my pants off, she shot the juice to that rig, and I fell out back of the camper in grass and soft sand."

"Did you get hurt?" Tamara asked.

"No," he said, "but I was standing in the highway in just my socks and drawers."

Tamara was now rolling in the middle of the bed laughing. "Grandaddy, tell me the rest of what happened."

"Well, you see, Camery, I felt my backside and my undershorts were split right down the back. Now, I am standing in the middle of US Highway 1 holding my shorts together with one hand and waving for one of those friends from the north driving a big car to stop and give me a ride. Two or three semis drove by and just blew their horn.

"About that time I looked up, heard a siren, and saw a blue light shining. A big Georgia State Highway patrolman was putting his hat on and walking toward me.

"'Mister,'" he asked, "'are you drunk?'

"'No, sir,'" I said, "'but if I could get a pint I would drink it. You see that camper going over the hill? Well, that's my wife, and we are going on a camping trip. I was tired and asked her to drive. I would get in the camper, pull off my shoes and pants, and about the time I got my pants off, she put the pedal to the metal and I fell out. Officer, if I hold my undershorts closed and ride with you, do you think you can catch that camper?'

"'I believe so,' he said.

"So he turned on the siren and blue light and stopped your Granny Bertie just before she got to where US 1 joins US 301 north of Folkston. The officer walked up to the car and said, 'Ma'am, where are you going?'

"She said she and her husband were going camping on the St. Mary's River.

"He asked, 'Where is he?'

"She said, 'In the camper sleeping.'

"The patrolman said, 'No, ma'am, he is in my patrol car and wants you to bring him his shoes and pants.'

"We thanked the kind officer, and I explained to your Granny Bertie what happened. We 'made up' and went on for a happy camping trip."

Her granddad asked, "Camery, do you know what I learned?"

"No."

"Never leave home with your underwear split all the way down the back."

There is another lesson we should all learn: nothing is much better than sharing a good laugh with a friend or family member. This is always uplifting. However, poking fun at another person's mistake or looks is downright rude and cruel. We need to know and respect the difference.

Take It

In my early career I learned a couple big lessons. One, people don't always say what they mean and mean what they say.

On February 14, 1957, I was discharged from the U.S. Army. My last assignment was at the Army Aviation School at Ft. Rucker, Alabama. The nationally and internationally known editor of *Flying* magazine, Richard Collins, was my flight instructor. A few months prior to discharge, I received my pilot's license.

My desire was to fly for a major airline. A few months prior to discharge, I met 1956 Miss Dale County, Alabama, "Maid of Cotton." She was a beauty and still is. I'm not sure what she saw in me, but I saw a lot in her.

My family had left the farm in South Georgia and moved to Jacksonville, Florida. Ed and I attended Jacksonville University after Mount Berry School for Boys in Rome later renamed Berry Academy.

I guess it made us look more important. We went to class four days a week and worked two days on campus and attended church, including Sunday school. Miss Martha Berry, the school's founder, had a good way to educate young people.

But it was great to be back in Jacksonville, after my Army service, and I looking forward to walking the aisle with Carolyn after a few "I do"s.

In the late fifties Jacksonville was called "the Little Hartford, Connecticut, of the South." Several very large life insurance companies gave it that name. I was employed by one of the largest companies, or at least they had the tallest building: the Independent Life. In those days much of the insurance was sold door-to-door. Likewise, there was a milkman, laundryman, furniture truck, rolling grocery store, coffee/tea man/woman, and the list goes on.

Very few people locked their house or auto doors. Most women were homemakers. In the rural area there would be an iceman who delivered 50- to 100-pound blocks of ice. Some say the "good ol' days," but I'm not so sure.

Mr. Eddie Knapp was my first manager. He knew more about people than most. During my first week on the job, I learned one of the great lessons of all time: "People don't always say what they mean or mean what they say."

In addition to collecting weekly and monthly premiums from policyholders, our assignment was to write and sell new policies.

Mr. Knapp took me to a dairy community in Marietta, Florida, ten miles west of Jacksonville. He had a prospect, Mrs. Sovona Moore's little baby boy, Tommy.

Little Tommy looked to be about two years old, and he was having his lunch the most natural way. I was raised on a little South Georgia farm in a community where most women fed their babies that natural way, even in church.

Mr. Knapp told Mrs. Moore we would come back later if it would be best. "Oh, no!" she said. "Tell me what I should buy for little Tommy."

Mr. Knapp explained the education plan to Mrs. Moore. He told about the advantage of little Tommy graduating from high school and going to a technical school, college, or university. Mrs. Moore wanted to save for little Tommy's education.

During the middle of the presentation, little Tommy decided he would not finish his meal. He pulled away, and she pulled him back. This became a back-and-forth between mother and child. At that time I did not realize I was going to learn the important lesson that people don't always say what they mean and mean what they say.

After about the third time little Tommy refused to finish his meal, Mrs. Moore said to him directly, "Take it, or I am going to give it to the insurance man."

The threat did not seem to bother little Tommy, but I said to her, "This is my manager, and he has seniority on me."

Uncle Dunk

Our farm was only three miles from highway US 1. I believe at that time it was paved from New England through New York to Miami and maybe to Key West.

It was fun to go to Mr. Smith's store on US 1. He sold gas and a few groceries and had a few tourist cabins. This was before Mr. Johnson and Mr. Wilson started building a Holiday Inn in Memphis.

We used to love to hear the folks from New York and Boston talk. They could fill up a big Buick for six dollars. If they had an extra empty seat in their car, it was mostly safe to pick up a hitchhiker.

When Ed and I were at Berry or when I was in the Army and in uniform, I could get home faster hitchhiking than buying a bus ticket. Boys and girls don't even think about this kind of travel anymore.

I guess Uncle Dunk (we never knew his real name) was tired of the snow up North and left his ride at Mr. Smith's store. He started walking to a farm on Market Road looking for work. Most farm families had a back room in their house and most of the time needed extra hands on the farm.

As far as I know, he always worked for Mr. Hutchinson. His wife, Miss Annie, was a good cook, and there was no reason to ever leave. Ed and I would ask him questions about where he lived up North—any questions just to hear him talk.

We never knew anything about his family. Uncle Dunk could never stand straight, about half bent over, but could outwork most of us.

Back then, there was a tradition in the rural South that a person who died would be buried the next day. Our friend and neighbor Mr. Walter Mattox would build a box casket and vault. Then the deceased would be laid to rest. (This all changed in the early 1930s.)

To pay tribute to the deceased, two or three men would sit up all night in the front room and drink coffee in front of the fireplace. My dad, Edgar Tillman, and two brothers from our community, Walter and Stanley Mattox, would "sit up," and other couples would come by to show their respect.

The deceased was usually laid out on a cooling board in a room across the hall. The door was left open. The body was covered, except for the face and head. Ed and I had to peek in when Uncle Dunk died.

As I said, Uncle Dunk could not stand straight. We never knew if it was from birth or maybe an accident. To keep him straight on the cooling board, a strong belt was tied around his feet and hooked under the table. Another strong belt wrapped around his chest. This kept him fairly straight for anyone who might want to make a respectful view of him.

By 10 p.m. everyone had gone home except Edgar, Walter, and Stanley. Around 11 p.m. Walter said, "Ed, if you and Stanley are going to 'sit up,' I think I will go on home. I have to get up early and finish the vault and casket."

"That's fine. We'll sit up.'"

About 12:30 a.m. Stanley said, "Ed, if you are going to 'sit up' all night, I'll go on home so I can help Walter early tomorrow morning."

"That's okay," he said. "I'm putting a new pot of coffee over the fireplace, and Uncle Dunk and I will be fine."

About 2 a.m. the worst storm anyone had seen in a long time hit. One big burst of lightning and thunder shook the whole house.

My dad looked across the hall. The chest belt had broken, and Uncle Dunk was sitting straight up on the cooling board. Edgar put his coffee cup down and said, "Uncle Dunk, if you are going to 'sit up,' I'm going home."

Old Man vs. Elderly Gentleman

It's been said that the big difference between an old man and an elderly gentleman is that the latter has money.

My friend Louis Barton and his family have had a funeral home in the small town of Adairsville, Georgia, for many years. The railroad station was the center of town and US 41 came smack through the middle of town.

The King sawmill was there when my dad spent a few of his early years in Adairsville. At that time there were no emergency medical services. Local funeral homes would take sick or injured people to the hospital.

Louis, as a young man working for his dad, answered an early morning call from an old man. The man told him his stomach was killing him. Louis must have completed a first aid medical course at Adairsville High. He asked the old man how long his stomach had been hurting.

"Ever since I have been up," the man replied, adding, "maybe since about six this morning."

Still probing for answers, Louis asked, "Have you had anything to eat?"

"No," the man said.

"Well," Louis continued, "have you had a BM today?"

"No," the old man said. "The only thing I have had is an RC and Moon Pie."

Laughter During a Dark Hour

Ed was a successful businessman in Jacksonville. Ed was a proud and happy man—married more than fifty years. He had two successful sons, who both married, and seven grandchildren. I spent most of the last year of his life with him.

I had gone from being a door-to-door salesman to vice president of a fine insurance company and then became assistant to the president of Berry College. I don't want you to think I was very smart, but I knew how to raise money. On a college campus that will make you important. It was great to see students receive scholarships who might not have been able to complete their college degree work otherwise.

I retired from both the insurance company and Berry College to spend nearly a year with Ed. Many nights, his wife, Carolyn, would move to another room and I would take their bed, which was next to a hospital bed.

His mind was good, and he had a positive attitude. During a procedure something went wrong, and he was paralyzed from his waist down. After that came a long period of rehabilitation. For several weeks the hospital let me move into the room with him in a sleeper chair and sometimes a cot.

Ed developed a friendship with the doctors, nurses, and other hospital staff. Even after he went home, some of the nurses would check on him. There was one nurse in training who had the duty of giving patients a bath. I'm not sure how long it takes, but after some time modesty is not in the room, or at least the patient and nurse do what has to be done.

The nurse's homeland was Argentina, and she had a beautiful accent. Ed and I still had our South Georgia farmboy accent. But we connected with her.

She loved country music and had a good singing voice. So we would close the hospital door and Ed would play the part of the announcer at the Grand Ole Opry. I played the part of all those in the audience when he would introduce her: "Now, let's make welcome Argentina's first lady of country music singing her latest hit, "Help Me Make It Through the Night!"

She would continue giving him his nightly bath and in her beautiful voice sing "Help Me Make It Through the Night." Sometimes Ed would roll his eyes at me. A year later, she came to Ed's funeral, and we gave her the special recognition she deserved.

The rehab people at the Brooks Medical Center in Jacksonville were really nice to us and let me push Ed's wheelchair to the rehab sessions. The folks really know how to prepare you for life after you leave the hospital. For example, each patient who needed a sliding board was given one. After some training you can slide off the bed to a chair and slide from a wheelchair to a car seat. I found out just how much a slick two-foot board could help.

Some of the therapy was done in a group setting. After several weeks Ed had become friends with most of the patients. The woman in charge made sure it was okay for me to be in the room. I believe there were a couple other caregivers or family members present. We sat behind our family members.

The leader, a young woman, was the consummate professional. It was obvious she had just received an advanced degree in group therapy. "Today," she said, "we want you to tell us why you are here or something about your life." But she said it was okay if someone didn't want to share.

There was an attractive woman present wearing several big diamonds that could have bought the hospital, one handsome coach, and the list goes on. All the patients were in wheelchairs. A horse had thrown one young lady; one young teenager had been injured in an auto accident; another patient, a middle-aged man, had been injured jumping into a swimming pool.

The young therapist looked at Ed and said, "Mr. Tillman, would you like to share?"

He rolled his eyes at me with a half-smile/grin. I thought, "Oh no! What's next?"

The group waited as he scanned the room, looking at each person in there with concern for what had happened to them. Ed was a master at captivating an audience—going all the way back to his sophomore year at Blackshear High School where he won second place in the speech contest.

He used to say that the only reason Cecil Cason won first place was because Cecil was better.

Looking straight at the therapist and then slowly at the others, he began to speak: "You see, I came home one night and caught my wife in bed with another man."

Now everyone was listening. Their favorite patient friend must have been in deep pain. He continued, "I rushed back outside, got my pistol, and started back to the bedroom. The man was a little shocked. He thought I was leaving when I went back to my car to get my pistol."

You could have heard a pin drop in the hospital conference room.

"As I came back in the bedroom, the man jumped out of the bed, took my pistol from me, and shot me. Now here I sit in a wheelchair with good friends."

"Oh! Mr. Tillman," the therapist said. "I never knew that. I'm so sorry."

"That's okay. Thank you for letting me share," Ed said. "What I just told you is not true, but I thought it might be more interesting than what really happened."

Most of the other patients by this time were laughing so hard they were about to fall out of their wheelchairs. The good-natured therapist knew she had been had but indicated it was one of her best sessions to see her patients laugh.

The hospital had a patient reunion a few months later and asked Ed to be their guest speaker. Most of the former patients were still in their wheelchairs but were learning to cope with life, learning to laugh. A patient called out, "Ed, tell us another story; we need a good laugh!"

One of the funniest sessions was when a staff member was teaching about how to avoid bed sores and sores from sitting the same way too long. A twenty-five-year-old teacher from forty miles south of Jacksonville who had been thrown from a horse and was now in a wheelchair and suffering from deep depression sat to Ed's left.

Her mother had asked Ed to cheer her up if he could. About halfway around the circle was the woman with all the diamonds who had her private hairdresser come every day. She was retirement age, but you could tell she did not rely on Medicare or Medicaid.

Human nature being what it is, we will pick on a person if they are too uppity. But we don't want them to know. This was a simple jester, no harm intended, and certainly top secret.

The leader said, "Sit up straight; push straight up." Ed rolled his eyes at me and looked at the young schoolteacher. I tried not to get ahead of him, but I knew the young teacher would be rolling in laughter in just a minute.

The leader said, "Now push up and lean to your right. Now push up and lean to your left." Ed would point toward the society lady where no one except the young schoolteacher could see him.

Each time to the right and then to the left, as he concealed his hand and pointed toward the lady, he had an air pocket grin on his face. I believe the hospital served beans before the session. By this time the young schoolteacher was laughing so hard she was about to fall out of her wheelchair. The teacher's mother told us the pep-up made her have some good days after that.

Close to the Last Ride

Ed had the gift of laughter. He expressed concern for those who took care of him when he was ill. But for the most part he had seventy years of good health.

He owned three car lots and sold 130 cars/trucks each month—totaling more than 30,000 automobiles sold in Jacksonville. He knew that after thousands of miles, a fan belt or a water pump would likely break. Sometimes our bodies will do the same.

Ed's heart had weakened, but he told his family it was just a bad cold. One evening, his breathing was not too good. His wife, Carolyn, called 911, and he was rushed to the hospital.

Carolyn called their two sons, and Stephen arrived at the hospital quickly. The doctor was checking Ed's blood pressure and heart rate and looking at Ed's medical chart. By this time Stephen was standing next to the bed. Ed had his eyes closed and seemed to be resting.

"Your Dad has had a couple heart attacks," the doctor said to Stephen. "If he has another one, do you want us to bring him back or just let him go peacefully?"

Stephen said, "Most certainly bring him back."

At that moment Ed opened his eyes, breathed a big sigh of relief, and said, "Thank you very much." He did live for several more months to enjoy his family and friends.

It is important to have a living will, giving medical staff and family permission to disconnect the tubes and unplug the power. That's not exactly how it works, but close enough. Even though this is a good thing to do, I have written in longhand below the signed will, "Please get a second opinion."

Family Laughter

Most of us have enough family members who have done interesting things or shared intriguing stories to provide family entertainment for a long time. I certainly have had such a family.

Uncle Hubert and Aunt Mattie were special. Most of us just called them Hubert and Mattie. They were successful farmers. They had good times and bad times. We mostly remember the good times.

They had three daughters and one son. We lived about a half-mile from them in the days prior to the Rural Electric Association.

You can have a good life without electricity, but it is inconvenient. Since we did not know any better, it was not a real problem.

Most country people cooked on wood stoves and got winter heat from a fireplace. I find it interesting now that we have two fireplaces in our house, mostly for show.

Hubert loved to back up to the fireplace, get real warm, and then run across the hall and jump in the bed. The room was dark, and everyone in the house knew where the bed was even without the lamp that provided light.

Mattie was a good housekeeper and always kept their home neat and enjoyable. Once, however, she did forget to tell Hubert she had rearranged the furniture in their bedroom.

The bed was moved to another corner of the room. Mattie knew what happened when she heard Hubert's knees and elbows hit the floor in the next room.

No Parking

My friend Gary Barton is really smart. He was a salesman for a computer company, owned a cabinet shop, sold insurance, and later became the agency director and vice president of State Mutual Insurance Company.

Gary drives 100 miles an hour when 50 might do just as well. He is a good family man and a graduate from the University of South Carolina who married a beautiful South Carolinian. They had one son, Dan, who is a Georgia Tech graduate and, like his father, very smart. Gary was a naval officer who did deep-sea diving.

Gary got in a big hurry one time. I asked Gary to relate the following story to us. Here's his account:

> Some years ago my job required me to travel around the country meeting with insurance agents. Occasionally, there would be large groups, and I would conduct training seminars. Usually these were uneventful. On a Monday or Tuesday I would drive from my home in Rome to the Atlanta airport, board a Delta Airlines flight to somewhere, and be met by our manager in whatever state I was visiting that particular week. We would check into the hotel where the seminar was scheduled to take place the next day.

The seminar would take place the following morning. We would have lunch, often with some of the seminar attendees, and then travel to another city and do the same thing there. On Thursday or Friday I would fly to Atlanta, retrieve my car, and drive home.

This story is not about one of those uneventful trips.

This time I was to go to Cedar Rapids, Iowa (or maybe it was Cedar Falls). That week, I was flying on TWA, which would leave from the opposite side of the airport from Delta, and I was running late.

In those days you were allowed to drive up to the curb at the terminal and leave your car long enough to carry your bags into the airport before moving your car to a parking area. Remember this; it's an important part of my story.

I stopped at the curb, rushed into the airport with my bags, and just made it to the gate in time to catch my flight. (If you noticed that I left out a necessary step in the procedure, you already have an insight into how this business trip developed.)

The next morning in Cedar Whatever, I conducted my seminar with a small group of ten to fifteen agents. Our state manager had arranged for a group lunch to be served in an adjacent meeting room. We sat around the table talking about the subject of the seminar and sharing personal anecdotes.

The conversation turned to the subject of my travel schedule, and I began to recount my process to the group. As I mentally reviewed the events of this particular trip, my mind arrived at the point where I had rushed from my car into the airport and…my car! I never moved my car from the curb!

I excused myself, went to my room, and started making telephone calls. I called everybody I could think of.

When I finally spoke with someone in the Atlanta airport security office, I learned that my car sat at the curb all day and part of the night before it was towed. While there, it was visited by an Atlanta police officer about once every hour, and it was ticketed. I learned that the police office in downtown Atlanta was responsible, so I called them.

Finally, I was routed to a sergeant who had heard about every story that could be fabricated. I told her my story. She was not sympathetic.

She told me that when I returned, I would need to come to the police station, pay my fine, and show proof of ownership. Then I could go to wherever my car was stored and pick it up.

Me: "But, Sergeant, I don't own the car."

Sergeant: "Who owns it?"

Me: "The company I work for."

Sergeant: "When you get home, go to the office, get proof of owner-ship, and bring it to me."

Me: "I live seventy miles away and need my car to get to the office."

Sergeant: "I *can't* let you have the car without proof of ownership."

Me: "Ma'am, would you please help me? I don't know what to do."

Sergeant: "Does your company have a fax machine?" (At this time fax machines were state-of-the-art, gee-whiz technological wonders, and our company had recently installed one.)

Me: "Yes, ma'am, but I have never used it."

Sergeant: "Well, call someone at your office who knows how to use it, have them fax me proof of ownership with verification that you have permission to be driving the car. When you get to Atlanta, come to the police station, ask for me, and I will help you get the car."

When I arrived at the Atlanta airport, I found an ATM machine, took out all the cash it would give me, and added it to the cash that was already in my wallet. I discovered a facility in the airport where I could store my luggage, hailed a cab, and headed to the police station.

Inside the police station I found a long line of other criminals waiting to speak to the police officer at the window. I got in line and waited my turn. When I got to the window, I did as the sergeant had instructed.

After I left the police station, I took another cab to the towing service. When I gave the cab driver the address, he said, "That's way out of town."

After a long drive we were in the open countryside and eventually came to the facility that had my car. Inside, I gave the owner of the facility the documentation from the police department, and he retrieved my car.

Finally, I headed back to the airport to get my bags. And, yes, I parked at the curb to go inside and fetch my luggage. Fortunately, there were no tickets and no towing this time. I can only imagine what the sergeant would have said if I had showed up with the same problem.

I drove home without any money in my wallet, but at least I had the car. In a meeting at the office a couple days later, I recounted this story to the howls of my colleagues. Dr. Steve Smith, chairman of the board, medical director, Rome aristocrat, and company autocrat said, "I don't think I would have told that."

Mount Berry School for Boys

It's hard to believe, but in 1902 there were only five public high schools in the state of Georgia. Several books have been written about Martha Berry, founder of the school that would later become one of the finest colleges in the country.

During the early part of the twentieth century, the Southeastern United States was mostly rural. In 1902 Berry taught reading, writing, and arithmetic. Not long after the founding of the boys school, President Teddy Roosevelt visited the campus and encouraged Miss Berry to start a girls school.

Later, she added a junior college and then a four-year college that still bears her name. Now, you can earn a master's degree there as well. Some have called it the "Harvard of the South." Most graduates will say not so—Harvard is the Berry of the North.

One hundred and sixteen years ago most students were taught to farm, build houses, or teach. Later, students majored in science, law, and medicine. Students became college professors, military leaders, ministers, and, most of all, good citizens.

Students attended class four days each week, worked two days, went to church on Sunday. Not a bad way to educate boys and girls.

Mr. Fred Loveday, our principal, and his wife, Mary, along with their two daughters, Nancy and Jean, became our parents, friends, and teachers.

Mr. Raymond Douglas, our basketball and track coach and teacher, helped mold young men to become successful in their professions and in business—as well as becoming good citizens, husbands, fathers, and church and community leaders.

Finding Humor in Unlikely Places

At one time Berry Schools had one of the finest hog farms in the country. I lived on a farm until I went to Berry at age seventeen.

Chester Hyers loved the hog farm and produced some of the best ham and pork chops in the country. Chester later married my first cousin Margaret, earning him the title "Cousin Chester."

For those who know a little about farming, the young male pigs have to be "marked." The marking causes the male pig to grow and mature in a wonderful way. It also prevents them from chasing the female pigs.

As you might know, the Future Farmers Club offered ribbons for outstanding club projects. Cousin Chester won the blue ribbon for being the best pig marker.

Each day at about 11:45 a.m., 200 high school boys would meet in front of Hill Dining Hall waiting for Cousin Chester to come to lunch from the hog farm. No one would say anything; they would stand straight and cross their hands in front of them. Sometimes you simply need to be quiet for a good laugh. The folks in Hollywood and New York call this situation comedy.

Redneck Pilot

A long time before Jeff Foxworthy was born, my granddaddy and uncles were telling redneck stories. Jeff was smart and made a career out of it. He says you should not make fun of a group of people unless you are one. Then he adds, "And I are one."

Well, I "are one" too. And to really enjoy and understand the redneck stories as they apply to a certain business, profession, or workplace, it's good to know something about the work people do.

Since I hold a commercial and flight instructor license and have taught many people to fly, here are a few redneck pilot jabs. You might be a redneck pilot if...

You use chicken houses for checkpoints.

Your cross-country flight plan uses flea markets as checkpoints.

You have mud flaps on your wheel pants.

You think "GPS" stands for "going perfectly straight."

You've ever used moonshine as Avgas.

Your toothpick keeps poking your mic.

You constantly confuse Beechcraft with Beechnut.

You have a black airplane with a big #3 on the side.

You use a Purina bag as a windsock.

You refer to flying in formation as "We've got ourselves a convoy."

Swimming Hole

In the South fifty to sixty years ago, some small towns and cities had nice swimming pools where boys and girls would meet. Parents felt their teens were well protected and could receive good exercise.

In the rural South the more rustic swimming holes were mostly for boys. Near our farm were excellent swimming holes at Hayes Lake, Bee

Lake, Mill Hole, or Hurst Lake. Even though they were called "lakes," they were mostly 300 feet long and 200 feet wide. Boys would walk or ride their horses or mules to the swimming hole for skinny-dipping.

We had a kind, gentle mule named Liz. One Saturday afternoon on a hot summer day, Ed and I hooked Ol' Liz to our wagon, and off we went to Hayes Lake, about a mile from our house. Several of our friends were already swimming there.

We undressed, threw our clothes in the wagon, and jumped into the swimming hole. We left Liz to graze on some of the new summer grass.

I don't know if you know much about mules or horses. The Lord gave them some kind of radar. When it gets late in the day, a mule or horse will go home.

We were having a big time at the lake, and more time passed than we realized. Ol' Liz went home with the wagon and our clothes. When our mother saw Liz and the wagon outside our house, she knew what had happened.

She left it to us to solve our problem. There were several large cornfields between the lake and our house. Leaving the main road, the cornstalks had their day with us. We finally made it home. But we still claim scars from that day at the swimming hole.

The next time, we made sure Ol' Liz was tied to a tree. And we learned an additional lesson: Never leave your clothes any place you can't get to them quickly.

Success While Failing

Most organizations talk about a positive attitude versus a negative attitude and success versus failure.

Several years ago, I was speaking to a group of insurance people in Indianapolis. Just prior to the speaking engagement, I read a book on the life of Eddie Fisher, one of America's great singing voices in the mid-1950s. He was to popular music what Elvis Presley was to rock and roll. One of his hits was called "Oh! My Papa."

I was expounding on the great truth of success in one part of our life and failure in the other part. Eddie married the beautiful Debbie Reynolds; the marriage failed. Then he married the exciting Elizabeth Taylor; the marriage failed. Then came Connie Stevens; that marriage failed too. One or two more, and they failed as well.

A man in the back of the room jumped up and yelled, "Hey, mister, he is doing better failing than we are succeeding."

That reminds me of the minister preaching his heart out and saying, "There was only one perfect person: Jesus. Do you know of another perfect person?"

A little man in the back of the church jumped out of his seat and said, "Yes, sir, my wife's first husband."

Sleepovers

When you are from a large family, cousins seem to enjoy visiting with each other. My parents, uncles, and aunts seem to always make room for two or three more to spend the night.

When we were small, we would sleep crossways on the bed. I told someone I had never slept by myself until after I got married.

Dr. Larry Atwell, retired superintendent of city schools in Rome knows lots of funny stories. His advice: "Don't put off until tomorrow anything you can delegate today." That might not break your ribs with laughter, but it is a great message.

I like my former pastor Dr. Floyd Roebuck's quote: "Most of the true stories I tell really happened."

A second-grade teacher related a story that might be a shocker if the mother knew. A girl in the class was telling her teacher about where she lived with her mother and the things they did and the dolls she slept with.

"Do you always sleep with your dolls?" the teacher asked.

"Oh, no," the little girl replied. "I usually sleep with my mama until the weekend when 'Uncle Charlie' comes over. Then I sleep just with my dolls."

Favorite Smart People

Our friends Chris and Ann Hook met at a community garage sale one evening when they were still fairly young.

Chris bought a chicken, a little pig, and a number three washtub. It was dark after the sale, and Chris asked Ann if he could walk her home.

Ann: "I don't know. When we get down the road, you might try to kiss me."

Chris: "How could I do that with this chicken, little pig, and number three washtub?"

Ann: "Well, I could hold the little pig, and we could put the chicken under the number three washtub."

Chris is a Delta captain. Ann is a nurse with a high position at a local hospital. They have two daughters, both University of Georgia graduates. Emily is working on her medical degree and Jessica is a physician's assistant.

So You Want to Be Somebody

My parents always told my siblings and me, "You are not better than other people, but you are as good as anybody you meet."

While Ed and I were in North Georgia attending Mt. Berry School for Boys near Rome, our family left our farm for the big city. Our sister, Jo, enrolled in Massey Business College in Jacksonville. Later, Ed and I enrolled in Jacksonville University.

We were moving on up. The family had a 1951 Chevy pickup truck and a 1949 blue Plymouth, a nice house, and most of the modern conveniences we had never had. People were buying new TVs; some had garage door openers.

Soon, the really important people were wearing beepers on their belt. Now the beeper was really something. Our doctors and volunteer firemen all had beepers. Church should have turned out after a doctor or volunteer fireman left the church. All the rest of us lost interest in the sermon until we found out what was going on down the street.

Ed and I really wanted to be somebody. We certainly could not afford a beeper, so we both got a garage door opener to wear on our belt. Our friends accepted it mostly as a joke, and for the most part it was. However, we impressed mostly ourselves.

Mother

My mother retired at the age of sixty-five from Slash Pine Community Action in Blackshear. Blackshear is a wonderful South Georgia town where people make a special effort to help others.

She taught people how to plant a garden, handed out food, took the elderly to the doctor, and made sure all the people had a good coat for winter. She had limited formal education but a PhD in experience and dedication.

A young woman from Atlanta with a master's degree in social work took her job when she retired. There seemed to be a little gleam in my mother's eye when she told about the well-educated city girl saying, "You can have this job; I'm going back to Atlanta."

She seemed to stand a little taller when the big boss from Waycross called and asked if she would return to work until the position was filled. She worked until the age of seventy. She found great humor in telling what happened to her.

The office was only six minutes from her house. A big traffic jam would be four pickup trucks and a car. The bell rang at 5:00 p.m., and in six minutes she was home and decided to take a short nap.

She woke up and looked at the clock. It was 7:30. "Oh my goodness, I will be late for work," she thought. That was a no-no in her day and certainly a poor example for the people she supervised.

At six minutes until 8:00 she was in her car going to work. As she turned right off Strickland Avenue, passed First Baptist Church and the county courthouse, things just did not seem right.

She hurried through the main traffic light, slowed down for the railroad track, and three minutes later unlocked her office door. Her office was in the old Blackshear High School—the stateliest building in town—converted into government offices.

No one else was in the building, and everything seemed darker than usual. She picked up the telephone and called one of her favorite nieces, Vera.

"You are not going to believe this," my mother said. "When I came through downtown, there were no cars, and the stores closed. I'm at work now, and no one is here—not even Mrs. Talley, the local vet's wife. It's getting darker. Vera, has the end of time come?"

Vera asked, "Aunt Bertie Mae, what time is it?"

Bertie Mae replied, "My clock says two minutes past eight. I got a good night's sleep and like to have been late for work."

"Aunt Bertie Mae," Vera said, "you took a short nap. It is 8:00 p.m., not 8:00 a.m."

They both laughed. Bertie Mae and Vera are now both in heaven now, and I wonder sometimes if they are still laughing about the time Aunt Bertie Mae was "late for work."

I Ain't Moved

Maybe it's poor grammar, but it's a good lesson. Recently, we were following a young couple. They were sitting so close together that it looked like one person driving the car.

It reminded me of the senior adult couple who observed a young couple during a Sunday afternoon drive. The woman said, "We used to sit like that."

Her husband replied, "I ain't moved."

Little Raise

Annually in our company, we visited with each employee and talked about how each might do a better job. Gina was a very good worker and one who would later become a company manager. It was my honor to review her progress.

Our president at the time, Dr. Steve Smith, did not have a reputation for giving big pay raises. I met with Gina to review and evaluate her progress. I said to Gina, "Dr. Smith asked me to thank and congratulate you for your good work but not to say anything about the little raise he was giving you."

It was confidential what people were paid, but everyone knew. Even Dr. Smith used to say the grapevine had never let him down.

I went back to Gina a second time with Dr. Smith's message. I thanked and congratulated her, then showed her the "little raise" and asked her not to say anything about it.

"Oh!" she said. "I won't tell. I'm as ashamed of it as he is."

The Ride of Paul Revere

On a walk through the campus of Harvard University, one of the great learning centers of the world, I was reminded of the ride of Paul Revere.

The story is told of Paul Revere and his fast ride through the countryside of New England on his speeding horse, yelling to the lady of the house, "Ma'am, is your husband home?"

"Yes," came the reply.

"Tell him the British are coming!"

Speeding to the next house: "Ma'am, is your husband home?"

"Yes," came the reply.

"Tell him the British are coming."

Racing to the next house: "Ma'am, is your husband home?"

"No."

"Whoa, horse!"

You might have to think on that one. If so, I'll slow down.

Borrowing Money

After college our son, Gary, worked with J. L. Todd Auction Company, a nationally known land auction company. He did not pursue this as a career, but became well known for helping raise thousands of dollars for schools, colleges, churches, and youth groups.

Gary later became founder and president of Gary Tillman Insurance Company and Aviation Insurance Brokers of North America.

One of the chants the student auctioneers learned carries an excellent message:

You have your money and your friend.
You loan your money to your friend.
You ask your money from your friend.
You lose your money and your friend.

My Uncle Harry was a very successful farmer. Now we call it agribusiness. When someone in the community wanted to borrow money from him, he would introduce them to Mr. Leo, his banker.

He said he had a contract with Mr. Leo that if Mr. Leo would not farm, he would not loan money. Remember, "Lose your money and your friend."

Mr. Waters had a better answer: "My wife and I decided a long time ago that we would not cosign or loan a relative or friend money without talking with each other."

A long time ago, I paid off a note that I cosigned with a coworker at our company credit union. It reminded me that experience is indeed a good education.

Remember not to lose money and a friend in the same transaction.

Some Failure, Lots of Success

We all fail at some point in our lives. The big problem with falling on our face or backside comes if we fail to get up.

An inventor once said he never failed; he just found hundreds of ways something would not work.

My brother and I both decided we were going to be doctors—until we took eighth-grade general science. Then we met our real Waterloo in ninth grade.

We had gone to a little country school in "the Forks of the Hurricane," correctly named because it was between Little Hurricane Creek and Big Hurricane Creek. From first through seventh grade, we met in a wonderful three-room school with one big room for joint meetings.

The big room was used for community activities and was perfect for events like a cakewalk or bobbing for apples at Halloween.

Also, we had a great basketball team in sixth and seventh grade. Our principal and coach, Mr. Roscoe Moore, was a great teacher. He taught good sportsmanship and the importance of doing our best.

Our first- through third-grade teacher, Mrs. Margaret Sweat, was a wonderful teacher. She had gone to college one or two years. I don't remember ever having a teacher who was a college graduate. In those days, 1930 to 1940, you could get a teacher's certificate if you graduated from high school or passed a state test.

The teachers were always studying to improve their skills. Most of the students continued to improve, becoming excellent homemakers, serving in the military, working for the paper mill or railroad, or farming. All was considered worthwhile work.

What the teachers said was considered to be gospel. Parents supported the teachers in whatever decision was made at school. I don't remember us ever having a so-called "problem student" in our school.

After seventh grade we rode a bus fifteen miles to school each day. It was not that far as the crow flies, but the bus driver also picked up children from Davis School, which added extra miles.

Many of the girls got married before they were eighteen, and the boys often quit school to farm. Ed, our cousin Lawanna Mattox, and I were the only three to graduate from high school in our class. I believe Ed and I were the first from our community or family to attend college.

It is amazing how things can change in one generation. Troops that came home after World War II and then the Korean Conflict often enrolled in a trade school, farm training program, college, or university. The GI Bill made a big difference in the life of many young men and women.

My uncles were part of the World War II group now referred to as "the greatest generation." I worked on my commercial pilot license on the Korean GI Bill. Our government got it right to help educate the troops after returning home.

Recently, an education leader in Georgia spoke to a community group I was in and indicated that now, perhaps more than at any time in many years, young people should seek a technical education. Many young people who receive college degrees now end up in debt for thousands of dollars.

My First Book

My first book was titled *How to Get a Raise or Promotion Without Asking: Making the Most of What You Make*. Sometimes you might connect better with the group or individual you are speaking to by using self-deprecation rather than expressing how great you are, so I often say, "The book was a bestseller. My cellar is full of them." It's amazing how many do not get the humor the first time around. Also, it might surprise you to find out just how many were or were not listening the first time.

Some families just don't joke very much and expect you to stick to the facts. My wife, Carolyn, is a good laugher. However, for her the story needs to have some meaning or border on correct information.

Early in our marriage, like most young couples, we never seemed to have enough money to pay all the bills. One day I came home and announced to her that the company was not paying us what we were worth. Then I added, "If they did, we could not live on it."

She took what I said seriously and said, "I knew something was not right." So to point out I was joking, I repeated, "We could not pay our bills if they paid us what we were worth." I found out she did not like humor that affected our family budget.

We had twenty-five agents (salespersons) in our office in 1957, and at the end of the year, I was the number one salesperson. Her response was, "A lot of these families are not doing so good." There is a big difference between number one and number twenty-five; just ask a high school or college coach.

Many people express a desire to do three things: write a book, pick a guitar, and fly an airplane. With the book and the airplane, I could help you, but I never could master the guitar.

Ed and I received a Gene Autry guitar when we were about thirteen years old. It came with a home study course. The only chords we ever learned were D7, C, and G. The picking part just never came. I have often wondered what would have happened if we had had a good guitar teacher.

We did try out for the Mt. Berry School for Boys Choir. Mrs. Lois King, the director said, "You boys need to stick to ushering."

A friend told me that most of us die with three good books in us. Even if you never write a book, let me encourage you to make some notes about some of your own goals, desires and aspirations. Learn and share your family history.

The older you get, the more your family history will mean to you. Talk with your mama, daddy, grandparents, aunts, uncles, and friends. Record the humorous and serious moments in your family.

At this writing I am happy to be eighty-five, born April 13, 1933. My brother and I were born at home in Valdosta, Georgia. There was no street address on my birth certificate. Twenty years ago, my mother could have given me that information. I am sure the house is long gone. It was a rental house.

At that time, my dad worked for the Atlanta Coal and Ice Company. Back then, the houses were heated with coal or wood and the ice for ice tea came from blocks of ice. I never knew much about this time in my parents' life.

Shortly after this time, my grandparents gave my family a 100-acre farm along Route 2 in Alma, Georgia. The gift had a stipulation: "You must live on the farm." Jo, Ed, and I spent the first seventeen years of our life on that farm.

There, we attended Beulah Baptist Church, Hurricane School through seventh grade, and Blackshear High School in Southeast Georgia. Such details in your own life may be of interest to your children and grandchildren, so please write them down.

One ol' South Georgia boy was looking for a way to avoid the draft during the Korean Conflict. When he reported for the health exam, he told the doctor to skip the exam, give him an M-1 rifle, and send him to fight: "Now. Not next week. Right now!"

The doctor said, "You are crazy."

The boy said, "Write it down. Write it down now."

⁕

Do You Know Much About Your Family?

Several years ago, a young professor at Union University in Jackson, Tennessee, suggested preparing a graph of our Christian growth. Family members will likely be interested in such information.

Sometime ago, I was doing an ethics seminar for a group of insurance people and suggested we list the five great religions of the world and see if each group had a code of ethics.

One young man named Southern Baptist, American Baptist, Free Will Baptist, and Hard Shell Baptist. Someone suggested he could stop because there may be twenty-eight different kinds of Baptist churches. Closer to the fact are Christianity, Judaism, Buddhism, Islam, and Hinduism.

Making a list of churches where you were a member and the civic clubs and companies you represented might give you and your family a guide to your growth as a person. I did this to pass along some information in case someone was interested:

Earl D. Tillman—Personal Guide

	Hometown	School/ Company	Church	Work
1933– 1938	Alma, GA	Childhood	Beulah	Farm
1938– 1947	Alma	Hurricane	Beulah	Farm
1947– 1950	Alma	Blackshear	Beulah	Farm
1950– 1952	Rome, GA	Mt. Berry School for Boys	Frost Chapel	Kitchen Crew Shop Library Farm
1952– 1954	Jacksonville, FL	Jacksonville University	Arlington Baptist	Shipyard

1954–1955	Gainesville, FL	University of Florida	First Baptist	University food & service
1955–1957	Ft. Gordon, GA; Ft. Jackson, SC; Ft. Monmouth, NJ; Ft. Rucker, AL	U.S. Army	Military chapel; First Baptist Enterprise	Foot soldier; personnel private to E-5 (Sgt.)
1957–1965	Jacksonville	Independent Life	Arlington	Agent; staff Manager
1965–1966	Chattanooga, TN	Independent Life	Oak Wood Baptist	Field trainer
1966–1970	Jackson, TN	Independent Life	First Baptist	District manager
1970–1973	Indianapolis (Carmel), IN	Herald Life	North Side Baptist	Division manager
1973–1974	Lexington, KY	Kentucky Central	Immanuel	Division manager
1974–2004	Rome	State Mutual	First Baptist	Vice president
2004–2005	Rome	Berry College	First Baptist	Assistant to president
2005–present	Rome	Tillman Aviation University	First Baptist	President

Bo's Prized Bull

Bo, who married our cousin Nadine, was a great South Alabama farmer. In addition to his row crop farming, he raised the finest beef cattle and hogs. He had learned the importance of blue ribbon breeding when he attended and graduated from Auburn University.

With that kind of background, Bo bought a bull. He put him in the field with several of his finest cows. The bull did not do what he was supposed to do, however, so Bo called the vet to come and check on his prize bull. The vet gave the bull (not Bo) a white and red pill.

During the next few weeks, the bull accepted his assignment and became the star of the pasture.

Cousin Tim stopped one day to find out why the great change in the bull's activity.

"Bo," Tim asked, "what did the vet give your prize bull?"

Bo replied, "I don't know, but it tasted like peppermint."

Pretty In and Out

For many years, we lived in a Navy town, Jacksonville. For several summers, when Ed and I attended Mt. Berry School for Boys in Rome, Jacksonville University, and the University of Florida, our main jobs were to work in the shipyards.

As the ships and aircraft carriers would come into port after six months at sea, the sailors would say, "There are no ugly girls on Saturday night."

I told my wife recently, "Carolyn, you just don't see any ugly young people anymore." I think of our own son, daughter, and granddaughters. Their mother received the best medical care. The children received regular checkups. As young people they had braces and good face cream.

But there's something more important than physical appearance. Most parents will make character-building statements to their children like, "Pretty is as pretty does." Interestingly, surveys reveal that many beauty contestants did not believe they were beautiful. I wish I had known that when I was in high school.

However, most of us know character is more important than the outside appearance. Hopefully that would have been the opinion of the contestants. My uncle said, "It is true beauty is only skin deep, but ugly goes all the way to the bone."

Don't Eat Your Seed Corn

While channel surfing the TV, I came upon a woman who was giving all kinds of financial advice. Most of it sounded pretty good. Some people called in asking if it was wise for them to buy a house, a boat, a motorcycle, a sailplane, or some other heart's desire. Most were discouraged from making such purposes because their current expenses exceeded their current income.

My Uncle Henry, a part-time preacher and broom salesman, would have said, "Spending more than you make just does not make good sense."

The other day, I looked at a fine ear of seed corn. Boiled and eaten off the cob, or cut from the cob, it would add to a fine meal. However, the ear of seed corn had 150 kernels. Each kernel could produce a stalk of corn.

Now we have 150 stalks, and each of those stalks could produce six ears. Then we could have 936 ears or 140,400 kernels—enough to feed our family and our neighborhood for many meals.

As Aunt Bessie said, "I do not believe in paying interest but earning interest." In other words, plant your seed corn; don't eat it.

Sharing the corn is also important. Our church teaches us to give ten percent of our income to help others. It is called the "tithe."

When Carolyn and I were just married, I asked Dr. Grady Snowden, "Should I tithe on my net or gross income?"

He said, "Earl, with what you make, it will not make much difference."

Rambling Thoughts

In February 1957 I was discharged from the U.S. Army with a new private pilot license in my pocket. My friend and flight instructor, Richard Collins, managed the Army flying club at Ft. Rucker, Alabama.

The flying club had both enlisted and Army officers. These were mostly officers not on flying status with the Army but who loved to fly.

The officers treated us with respect, but we were always aware of the stripes versus the gold or silver bars or clusters. Deep down inside I always wished I had taken ROTC or gone to officer candidate school.

After my tour of duty, I returned to the business world, which had a similar order. Instead of enlisted and officers, we had salesmen and managers. Since it seemed the managers, like officers, drove pretty cars and lived in beautiful houses, I wanted to be one of them. It is interesting how we build up insecurity in our mind that really has nothing to do with the other person.

In the mid-1950s a person could buy a good training or personal airplane for $1,500 to $2,000. For example, an Aeronca Champ-7AC, an Aeronca Chief 11AC, an Ercoupe 415C, a J-3 Cub, or a Taylor Craft could be bought for about $1,800.

These same planes now cost between $20,000 and $40,000. Recently, I updated my Cessna 182RG with a Garmin 530, new audio panel, and S-Tec 30 autopilot. The avionics shop is $35,000 happier.

The idea of flying might not sound like a big deal to some people. But for a South Georgia boy who spent most of his boyhood days looking at the backside of a southbound mule, it's a big deal.

It All Has to Do with Rank

Miss Martha Berry invited President Teddy Roosevelt to visit her boys school near Rome. The school that began in 1902 was founded for mountain boys with little opportunity for an education.

In 1909 President Roosevelt visited her school and encouraged her to organize a girls school, which she did. Sometime later she was quoted as saying she would have started the girls school first if she had known how much the boys could eat.

Recently, I was reminded of what I learned about President Teddy Roosevelt's son who became a general. A young service man was standing at the ticket counter trying to get a ticket to go see his sick mother. The ticket agent explained to the young service man that all seats were taken.

General Teddy Roosevelt Jr. overheard the conversation, stepped out of line, and told the ticket agent to give the young serviceman his seat.

"But you are a general," the ticket agent said.

"Yes," replied General Roosevelt. "It all has to do with rank. I am just a general, and he is a son."

Special Notes

Forty-four days prior to his death, Ed gave me a book with a special note. The book was a biography of the billionaire Howard Hughes, a great pilot and movie producer who could never get it quite right with his personal life.

Ed's note, dated August 19, 2005, reads, "To my brother Earl...who stood by me when the nurse's station sent out the alarm 'code blue' and the doctors prepared to remove the ventilator. He visited me in the time of loneliness. To Earl and his wife Carolyn, I will always be grateful.

May this book be a blessing as you soar through the skies. Love and Best Wishes, Ed."

Notes are important. Have you written or received one recently?

Every Tub Must Sit on Its Own Bottom

You must have heard your parents or grandparents expound on great truths for living. In the modern computer age you might say, "Garbage in, garbage out."

Some young folks might say I really want a college education, but my folks can't send me to college. You might not be able to go to Harvard or Yale or even Emory. Go to a community college or apply for work scholarship at Berry College. There are some opportunities in getting an education online as well.

There are a lot of years between ages eighteen and seventy-five. Don't blame someone else for what happens during that time. Someone said they would be thirty years old before they could complete the degree they wanted. The classic response is, "And how old will you be if you don't?"

There are old sayings with lots of truth: "Each tub must sit on its own bottom" and "You have to sleep in the bed you make."

Much of what happens in our lives is of our own initiative and commitment.

Too Big, Too Fast

I agree with my granddad that farmers were born to farm, carpenters were born to build, and teachers were born to teach. Include your occupation and you have the idea, with maybe one or two exceptions.

Having lived my early years on a 100-acre South Georgia farm, I could never understand why the government wanted to pay farmers not to farm. With hungry people all over the world, why not pay and pay well for production, not non-production?

With tongue in cheek I remember Cousin Charles and Cousin Edward cashing in on a government program.

Charles: "Let's get some of that non-production government money."

Edward: "What should we not grow?"

Charles: "You know a lot about hogs, so let's not grow hogs."

Edward: "Great idea. How many should we not grow?"

Charles: "Let's not grow fifty head this year."

After receiving their government check the first year, things seemed to be going great, so Edward asked, "How many should we not grow the second year?"

Charles: "Let's not grow a hundred head."

They signed up at the local government office and got their check. Then the third year came around.

Edward: "How many hogs should we not grow?"

Charles: "Let's not grow 150 head."

They went for their payment but discovered the government office had stopped their check. Cousin Charles surmised, "I guess we just got too big, too fast."

It's a funny story but one that leads to a serious question for me: Why not pay farmers to produce food and feed hungry people?

Don't Need to Be Healed Today

Be careful what you ask for today; you might get it.

My channel changing drives my wife crazy unless I land for a while on one of the cooking or home decorating programs she likes. Recently, I paused on a church program.

People were mostly jumping up and down, with some shouting and lots of "Amens." In a few minutes the organ hit a couple notes that matched the rhythm of the minister's speaking voice. I knew then it was time to forget about the rest of Dr. Phil and Paula Deen's cooking and just watch what was about to happen.

Folks were lining up for some ol' fashioned healing. Someone yelled, "The Spirit is moving." It reminded me of Robert Duvall in his award-winning movie *The Apostle*.

One man came across the stage with a neck brace, saying, "Pray for me, but don't touch my neck brace. My accident case does not come up for two weeks."

It reminded me of the time someone asked for prayer for his hearing. The preacher slapped both ears and asked, "Now how is your hearing?"

The man replied, "I don't know; it's not until next Thursday."

Who Was It?

An altar boy from Blackshear, nine miles east of Waycross, went to see the priest. "Father, I have sinned," he confessed.

"With whom?" asked the priest (who must've had Martha Harrison for his English teacher).

"I can't tell," said the youngster.

Prodding him toward deeper confession, the priest asked, "Was it Hattie Merrill?"

"I can't tell," the altar boy said a second time.

"Well," the priest asked, "was it Annie Maude?"

Again the boy responded, "I can't tell."

The priest said, "Well then, young man, you cannot serve as an altar boy for three months."

The young lad's friend was eagerly waiting outside. He asked his buddy, "What did the priest say?"

The boy said, "He gave me a three-month vacation and two good prospects."

It's Okay to Get Emotional

"Big boys don't cry" is a statement most of us have heard. Don't believe it.

Recently, I flew Lynn Dempsey and his son Gaines to St. Simon's Island, Georgia, to join Ray, chairman of the board of the prominent Dempsey Auction Company. Wives, children, and grandchildren were all there for the Georgia State Auctioneers meeting to witness Ray's son Lou's induction as the state president of the Georgia State Auctioneers Society.

Joe Tarpley, longtime president of J. L. Todd Auction Company, was also there. Since this writing Gaines is the president of the Georgia auctioneers.

The Dempsey family has the gift of laughter and a positive attitude that would make any organization proud. Katie, Lynn's wife and Gaines's mother, is one of the best Georgia state legislators.

In addition to Lou taking the leadership of the association, an auctioneer was named to the hall of fame for their profession.

The speaker started with something like, "This is your life." He choked up, stopped to gain his composure, and then with a little self-deprecation said, "Don't mind me. I get emotional watching reruns of *Lassie*."

Trying to prompt some laughter, I mentioned that I have seen *Gone with the Wind* eighteen times and still get emotional before the ticket is torn. But to remember *Lassie* was tops.

So, men and boys, go ahead and shed a few tears now and then. A good cry is as healthy for you as a good laugh.

Just Trying to Do Good

An undertaker called the church requesting a young minister to conduct a graveside service eight miles from town in a rural section of the county. It was for a homeless man who had no family members or friends present.

The undertaker suggested that a brief Scripture reading and prayer would be sufficient. A young minister agreed to the ministry opportunity and scribbled down directions.

He got off track and was running very late when he finally came upon two men sitting patiently on a big pile of dirt. The young minister thought it only right to read the selected scripture and offer a prayer—which seemed to be extra long and loud.

Having fulfilled his spiritual duty, the young minister drove away. One of the men still sitting on the big pile of dirt with shovel in hand said to the other, "You know that was the best and only prayer I have ever heard over a new septic tank."

Best to know where you are going and when you get there.

Eye Doctor

Rome has been recognized nationally for its excellent medical community. We are blessed to have so many great medical people here.

The traffic just got too busy for us to go to Atlanta, Chattanooga, or Birmingham for medical care. Now the local Harbin Clinic alone has more than 150 doctors. The Rome community really has two fine hospitals and other excellent medical services—as well as local colleges that train nurses and dental professionals.

I still have a problem knowing the correct name between the foot doctor and the eye doctor. I do know my cousin Dr. Rick Tillman in Carrollton, Georgia, is an optometrist, or OD. Even the phonebook lists it that way, which is good because, if not, Cousin Fred and I may get mixed up and go to the obstetrics office.

Recently, I went to our ophthalmologist. The assistant was doing the eye test before the doctor came in. The questions bother me sometimes because it's hard to keep up.

She asked, "Which is better: one or two?"

I was scared I would give her the wrong answer, so I asked if she ever tricked the patient to see if the answer was remotely correct. She said sometimes one and two might be the same.

She told me of a recent exam she had conducted. After asking which one was better, the patient replied, "Honey, which one do you think is best?"

Same Condition, Different Pronunciation

When I was discharged from the U.S. Army in February 1957, I was two months away from marrying the love of my life. I needed a civilian job—and fast.

My family had moved from a small South Georgia farm to Jacksonville. I was ready to make it big in the business world. The best job I could find was a door-to-door insurance salesman position.

Just prior to my discharge, I received my private pilot license and was studying for my commercial license on the Korean GI Bill. The airline jobs were pretty well taken by ex-Air Force, Navy, and Marine pilots. At that time most of the ex-Army pilots had flown helicopters or small observation aircraft.

My future bride, Carolyn, had just won the title of "Miss Maid of Cotton, Dale County, Alabama." Plus, she had won third place in the 4-H Club biscuit-making contest. She had already said "Yes" to the marriage question.

I needed a job before she had time to reconsider her answer. Back in those days, future mothers-in-law did not look too fondly on young men who were not gainfully employed. Long story short, I did not have time to look for the so-called "perfect job."

To be a good door-to-door salesperson requires a high tolerance for pain. I soon learned some of the great lessons of all time.

The first was that when a woman tells you her dog won't bite, what she really means is her dog will not bite her.

On an early Monday morning, my supervisor, Mr. Eddie Knapp, took me to the field (which wasn't really a field but a nice neighborhood in Marietta, now part of Jacksonville). Mrs. Joann Anderson was our first prospect.

There are lots of medical questions on the application for life insurance. Even fifty years ago, there were questions you had to ask without killing the sale but still getting the information the company needed to properly underwrite the risk.

However, one should never ask a woman how old she is, so Mr. Knapp would ask her birthdate or the year she was born (and it's better to guess at weight after you get back in the car). Many medical words we could never spell, so we had to look them up in the medical book. (Doctors probably can't spell them either. That's likely why they write the way they do.)

Back then, it was not customary for men to talk with women they did not know about what was considered personal (this was before Dr. Ruth or Dr. Phil), so we simply asked Mrs. Anderson if she had ever been in the hospital.

"Yes," she replied.

"For what reason?"

"I had one of *those* operations."

"Oh! Was it a female operation?"

"Yes."

We knew the underwriter would want to know if the procedure was "total" or "partial."

"Total," she said. "I had a total wreck-to-heck-to-me."

Mrs. Anderson signed the application, paid the premium, and seven days later we presented her with a life insurance policy. The day of the sale, Mr. Knapp told me what operation she had from his little medical book and how to spell it.

From that first day of a door-to-door salesman to becoming vice president, the insurance business was pretty good. Carolyn and I had the good fortune to raise a fine son and daughter who both received a college education. Miss Berry, the founder of Berry College, said, "All good work is honorable."

Fast forward to the year 2018 and many college graduates will tell you they would just like to have a job—even going door-to-door.

Remembering Too Much

Several months ago, Beth gave Cousin Margaret a big birthday party in Waycross, Georgia. Many from her 1955 Blackshear High School graduating class were there.

Margaret, a beautiful cheerleader for the Fighting Tigers, learned to play the piano and could drive a tractor on her family farm by the time she was ten years old. Most of our cousins were there.

There was some caution among the guests about what would be said over the speaker system since her pastor from Beulah Baptist Church was there. I suspect he had heard enough in his career not to be shocked.

Gene Davis, a longtime friend, and his country band were there. In high school they were the number one FFA (Future Farmers of America) group in Georgia. Gene can tear up a piano and make most piano players in Nashville look like Ned in the first reader. It's amazing how folks can have a good time with food and nothing stronger than iced tea and lemonade.

I shared a story that had become "fact" over time. As I remembered, on Margaret and Chester's wedding night she went to bed early, still in her traveling clothes. When questioned why she would go to bed with her traveling clothes still on, she said, "Aunt Bertie Mae said Chester and I would be going to town by 9:30 p.m."

Bertie Mae Peacock Tillman, my mother, had the gift of laughter. One prank she loved was to "short sheet" the bed. I am not sure how that all works, but sewing the sheets in the middle caused the newlyweds some problem getting in the bed. In those days no young bride would come to bed unless the lights were out. So the "short sheet" prank was long remembered.

The U.S. Army

During my third year at the University of Florida (1954–1955), I took accounting and statistics, not two of my better subjects. If you were not in ROTC or the upper third of your class, the university sent the draft board a note. In those days all young men at age eighteen were required to register for the draft. In hindsight I should have made better grades. Some of the young men were accused of taking underwater basket weaving to improve their grade point averages and avoid the Army draft.

On February 14, 1955, I reported to the U.S. Army induction center. Shortly thereafter and for the next two years, I served at Ft. Jackson, South Carolina; Ft. Gordon, Georgia; Ft. Monmouth, New Jersey; and Ft. Rucker, Alabama.

I loved Ft. Monmouth, which was not too far from New York City. World War II had ended nine years earlier, and the Korean Conflict was winding down. Lots of us bragged about having the best outfit in the U.S. Army, and the North Koreans heard we were coming, so they wanted to stop fighting before we got there.

Today, as our young men and women return from Afghanistan or any place of service, we thank them for their service to our country. The same was true in my time. Soldiers would put on dress uniforms and go to New York City. We were invited without charge to the New York City Music Hall. For the first time I saw the Rockettes kicking their heels high in the air. I had never seen anything on the farm that could kick that high.

A friend of mine who had lived and gone to school in Brooklyn invited me to go to Coney Island with him. That was the first time I had eaten a pizza. Asbury Park, New Jersey, was the country club of the Army. What we called "going to the beach" down South was called "going to the shore" in New Jersey. I'd never seen so many good-looking girls.

After a tour of duty at Ft. Monmouth, I was transferred to Ft. Rucker, Alabama, only about sixty miles from Panama City Beach. Come to think of it, the Georgia, Alabama, and Florida girls were just as beautiful as those we met in New York and New Jersey. They just talked a little differently.

Ft. Rucker is where I met Carolyn and learned to fly. We really met at the First Baptist Church in Enterprise, Alabama. She was a civil service employee for the U.S. Army.

A Sixty-One-Year Love Affair

At this writing Carolyn and I have had a sixty-one-year love affair. Mostly we've shared happy times. We lost our parents, grandparents, uncles, aunts, cousins, my twin brother, sister, and close friends.

After losing our son, Gary, when he was still a fairly young father and our granddaughter, Hannah, when she was in the prime of her youth at age sixteen, we were left to wonder "why."

Some people said, "They are in a better place." Maybe true, but I found no comfort in that statement. There were questions about heaven that no one seemed to be able to answer. I will talk more about this a bit later, but to say they are in a better place just did not bring me much comfort.

The kind folks who said they loved Gary and Hannah and they were thinking of us seemed to bring the most comfort. We do believe in heaven, and knowing they both had accepted Jesus Christ is a comfort.

Sharing laughter about the good times we all had together has provided us comfort as well. Twelve years have passed, and the laughter we share keeps the good memories alive.

How It All Started

A good question for a young married couple is, "How did you meet?" The answers are interesting. Some will say they met at a cousin's wedding or through a friend or relative. Some met on the Internet or in a bar.

Sometimes you still hear of people meeting at church. Church often does a good job of providing good social activities as well as worship and other spiritual experiences.

One of the biggest events in Southeast Alabama near Ft. Rucker was the annual Peanut Festival. Sometimes a big movie star like Roy Rogers, Gene Autry, or Johnny Mack Brown would ride his horse in the parade.

Johnny Mack Brown was a football player at the University of Alabama. After playing in the Rose Bowl, he went back to California and became a cowboy movie star. He was not as well known as Roy and Gene, but he was a native son who could draw a crowd for a parade in Alabama.

High-stepping majorettes appeared with their high school bands following. The Army participated with Jeeps, a tank, and some aircraft on trucks. This was a day to remember.

Somehow, I qualified for the U.S. Army Honor Guard. We had two soldiers carrying the flags and two carrying M-1 rifles. The Honor Guard led the entire parade.

I was the soldier on the left carrying the M-1 rifle as we headed west on Main Street. The bands were playing all the current military tunes, and old vets on the street corner were standing with a smart salute to the flag with some special memories of days gone by.

As we passed the local drugstore on the corner, First Lt. Steve Berry came to a smart salute and whispered to his date, "The soldier on the left with the M-1 rifle is my friend Earl Tillman. We are in the Ft. Rucker Army Flying Club."

Somehow, Steve had a good memory for birthdates. "Carolyn," he said, "you and Earl have the same birthday, April 13." I have been reminded a few times that it may be the same day but with four years between.

Steve went through ROTC at Stetson University in Deland, Florida, and was part of their music program. He had a good voice, and Carolyn loves to sing. She always claimed they were just good friends.

My off-base church while stationed at Ft. Rucker was the First Baptist Church of Enterprise, Alabama, famously known for its monument to the boll weevil. That's a story all by itself: South Alabama farmers grew cotton to clothe and feed their family. But the boll weevil destroyed their crops year after year, so they started planting peanuts. They did so much better with the peanuts than with their cotton. The monument was their way of thanking the boll weevil.

Meeting Future Wife

Most of the unmarried soldiers who attended First Baptist Church of Enterprise, Alabama, joined the Sunday evening choir, mostly because that was where all the girls were.

Steve and Carolyn were invited to sing in the youth choir in Enterprise. Steve and I sat on the third row behind Carolyn. At that time I did not know Steve had spoken kindly to Carolyn about our flying club and that we both had the same birthday. I whispered to Steve, "Not bad."

Ed and I had a 1954 Chevy. He had it with him at the University of Florida in Gainesville, so I had to get a ride the best way I could. Unlike today, more young men did not have a car than did.

I asked Steve for a ride back to Ft. Rucker before he took Carolyn home. We stopped at Bondy's for a Coke and hamburger. Carolyn and Steve told me she worked at Troop Supply, which kept the records on the military equipment and parts.

Sometimes the Lord is good to you if you act right. Some would call it good luck and others an answered prayer. Monday morning, the Army sent Steve to Ft. Benning near Columbus, Georgia, for some minor throat surgery. In those days most hospital stays lasted at least a week.

It just did not seem right not to call Carolyn and thank her for going to the big parade and visiting First Baptist with Steve. Since we were both back at Ft. Rucker, a more formal call was in order.

"Miss Bagwell," I said when Carolyn answered, "this is Specialist Tillman here." I'm not sure of her reply, but I thought it only proper to invite her to dinner at Gabe's Fish House in Dothan. She liked the idea, and I borrowed my flight instructor Richard Collins' Packard.

I don't remember much about the fish, but I never went out with another girl after that date. I called Ed and told him of meeting Carolyn and that I needed our car.

Carolyn and I saw each other nearly every day for six months. I would eat lunch at the Army mess hall, and she usually brought a sandwich from home. We would park under a big oak tree and talk during her lunch break.

She and her family were active at Spring Hill Methodist Church. Come to think of it, I don't remember ever going back to First Baptist, Enterprise, after that.

Fifteen years later, I met Brady Justice Jr. at Northside Baptist Church in Indianapolis. I asked Brady if he knew a Dr. Justice who was pastor at First Baptist, Enterprise, Alabama. He said, "Yes, that's my dad."

Carolyn and I dated for six months. So much for long engagements. I took off work one Friday, and we married at First Methodist Church of Newton, Alabama, on Saturday. Then we drove to Jacksonville on Sunday, and I went back to work on Monday. I can't say much for a two-day honeymoon, but the sixty-one years of marriage have been great.

❖

Joyce

Joyce is one of South Carolina's finest women. A dedicated teacher, Joyce once took eighteen graduating seniors on a cruise. She and her sister Joann, also a retired teacher, have the gift of laughter.

I was told some of the best humor comes from the beauty shop. On one visit to the beauty shop, Joyce's stylist asked, "Joyce, how are you doing?"

Joyce replied, "I am so tired, I don't know my head from my rear end."

"Well," the stylist said, "you better decide pretty quickly, because I am going to shampoo one of them."

Gift of Tongues

In the South, we have Methodists, who believe sprinkling is good; Baptists, who believe in immersion; Presbyterians, who dress well and are educated; Episcopalians, who drink in front of each other (Dr. Smith used to say they were Catholics who flunked Latin).

The Seventh-Day Adventists have it worked out where they can go to church on Saturday and get the day off on Sunday. Our longtime Christian education director at First Baptist Church of Rome, Bill Davies, talks about doing away with the U.S. Post Office delivery and letting the Jehovah's Witnesses and Latter-Day Saints bring the mail since they're going out to houses anyway.

These comments are meant in jest as a way of not taking ourselves too seriously. Those who make it will all be together in heaven. We won't have to defend any belief "up there." It would take several books to pick on all of us.

In our part of the world, the Pentecostals seem to know how to really enjoy their religion. Recently, our Sunday school class studied the "gifts of the Spirit." Most seem to understand the gift of sharing, the gift of music, and the gift of healing.

Then the subject finally got around to the gift of speaking in tongues. None of the eighteen in the class of senior adult men had the gift of tongue. But most had Pentecostal friends and had witnessed their gift on tongues.

My longtime friend and a Pentecostal minister, Dr. Ken Edenfield, was always quick to remind his flock that the gift of speaking in tongues was not the greatest gift of the Spirit. That would be love.

Grammar

A woman who lived about halfway between the Northwest Georgia communities of Coosa and Armuchee had a major goal in her life: to send her daughter to college. She worked two jobs and saved, saved, saved for her daughter's education.

The big day came, and the mother was so happy when her daughter left home for college. At the end of the first semester, her daughter came home for a family reunion.

In a quiet moment in a private room, the daughter confessed, "Mama, I ain't no virgin no more."

The mother replied, "After all I have done to send you to college and you are still saying 'ain't'?"

Hearing Loss

My Aunt Bert just loved her minister. "He visits me when I can't go to church," she said. "And he has wonderful sermons, but I can't hear a word he says."

My friend Dr. Jack Runninger told me of a man who was so proud of his new hearing aid. He said, "It restored my hearing."

Jack asked, "What kind is it?"

His friend replied, "Oh, it's about twenty minutes 'til two."

Most of us know the questions to expect during our regular medical exams. However, the doctor sometimes talks in shorthand.

"Big breaths," he said to one woman, who proudly responded, "Thanks. You should have seen them forty years ago."

While examining one man, the doctor was surprised to find a suppository in his ear. But the news brought joy to the man: "Well, thank the Lord. Now I know where my hearing aid is."

Same Word, Different Meaning

People talk more openly about personal matters now than they did long ago. I liked the older custom better.

A husband and wife were asking me about Carolyn. So I mentioned that she was much better since her implant.

They perked up and said, "Oh! She did not seem to need an implant."

I said, "Well, I am not sure if she did or not, but she seems to be chewing her food much better."

Writing and Talking

After flunking freshman English, I spent a whole summer studying 159 rules of good grammar. However, I still find it easy to leave the "-ing" off of many words.

Often I ask Carolyn to spell a word for me. My friend Merrill Davies, a grammar expert, retired teacher, and author of several books, told me kindly, "Earl, you write just like you talk."

It was kind but not necessarily a compliment.

Quiet Is Better

Many times, just being quiet is better. We were taught this in most of our marketing classes. The managers and the university professors gave lots of good reasons for quiet time.

Most young mothers teach their children to be quiet and to listen. But we don't practice what we preach. My side of the family is on automatic talk mode when we get up in the morning.

Sometimes at family get-togethers we all talk at the same time. My wife's family is much better at just sitting in front of the fire during the winter months, sometimes grunting or chuckling.

During summer, sitting on the front porch enjoying the breeze, someone might say, "Look, there goes a hawk."

There's a time to talk and a time to be quiet. When in doubt, being quiet is often better.

Saturday at the High Rise

One Saturday while visiting members of the high rise Sunday school class, one woman told me she did not have any friends. I asked if she had a telephone, and she said, "You know I do."

"Would you do me a favor next week?" I asked. "Do you know ten other ladies?"

She said, "You know I do."

I suggested, "Make a list of ten people you know, and call them. Ask about their grandchildren, and then just listen."

The next week, I asked her how it went. She said she had made the calls and listened and listened and listened.

Then she said, "I am not sure I need friends that much."

The Hiding Composer

To earn kindergarten tuition fees for our son and daughter, Carolyn taught music. One class was about the composer Joseph Haydn.

After returning home, Gary asked, "Mother, why was Joseph hidin'?"

Punctuality

Waycross, Georgia, was a big railroad town when I was a child. Uncle Smitty, a railroad man, would visit us in the country. Nieces and nephews would gather around him to see his big watch.

I still remember him telling about the importance of being at work on time and the trains being on schedule. Being on time in your business or profession is nearly as important as your product, knowledge, or skill.

Neither Delta nor Greyhound will wait on you if you're late.

Mail Plane

From the 1930s to the 1950s, someone told us the mail plane came over our farm every day at 11:30 a.m. I later learned it was a DC-3 out of Atlanta with stops in Macon and then Jacksonville.

Even back then, I thought flying high in the sky must be a lot more fun than plowing Ol' Mary and Ol' Gray (I never did know why we called them "Ol'"). We knew after the mail plane flew over, it was soon time for a good lunch our mother had prepared.

In the past fifty years I have flown that same route many times, from Rome to Atlanta to Macon and then Jacksonville. I will usually rock my wings a couple times at the farm and remember the lessons learned on that small South Georgia land.

Family Talk

Being twins, my brother and I hardly ever used the words *me*, *mine*, or *I*. It was always *our* uncle, *our* aunt, *our* grandparents, *our* mama, *our* daddy.

Our dad was the oldest of seven children. In 1922 he ran away from home at age sixteen and rode a freight train across Georgia from Waycross to Adairsville, near Rome.

He had completed seventh grade, the highest class taught at the Hurricane School at the time. He never viewed his departure as running away, but just wanting to see more of the world.

While working at the saw mill for the King family, they encouraged him to go to the Berry School. They told him he could work two days and go to school four days for his education.

He didn't go but never forgot their advice. So when Ed and I were sixteen, he took us from our South Georgia farm to Berry. At that time I could have never imagined that one day I would have the title "assistant to the president."

Today, the King family saw mill is long gone, but grandson Evan King is the mayor of Adairsville. The Kings are members of First Baptist in Rome with us, and we enjoy visiting in their home.

After our dad left the saw mill, he returned home and then joined the U.S. Army for three years. After his Army days he returned home again and married the farm girl next door. Then came our sister, Jo, then Ed and me.

In December 1941 our dad was on a merchant ship two days out of Glasgow, Scotland. The German submarines were blowing up every merchant ship they could find. He was lucky his ship made it back to Savannah, and he came home to farm and work in the shipyard in Brunswick, Georgia, during the remainder of WWII.

Even though he had very little formal education, he had access to a good library on the ships, and he loved to read and wanted us to have a better education than he had received.

Our Sunday school at Beulah Baptist Church met at 4:00 p.m. every Sunday. Dad made Ed and me study our Sunday school lesson and then stand in front of him and teach the lesson. We hated doing this, but for the most part we were better prepared.

That training later proved very helpful to us. At Blackshear High School, Ed won second place and I won third place in the speaking contest. Then, in our senior year at Mt. Berry School for Boys, I won first place and a ten-dollar gift.

In May 1952 both Aunt Bert and Aunt Sallie sent us ten dollars each for graduation presents. That might not sound like much, but the speaking gift and graduation gift were enough for us to buy a Greyhound ticket from Rome to Jacksonville, where we enrolled in Jacksonville University. Our dad never said much about it, but he had some pride that his boys were the first from our family to attend college.

Our daughter, Tamara, received a diploma from West Rome High School, a degree in early childhood education from Samford University, and a master's degree in religious education from Southern Baptist Theological Seminary in Louisville.

Our son, Gary, received his college degree from Cumberland University in Williamsburg, Kentucky, where he was an all-American in indoor and outdoor track. He spent his first year at the University of Georgia. Football coach and athletic director Vince Dooley came to Rome to present Gary with his Bulldog letter.

A year after his untimely accident, Gary was inducted into the Rome athletic hall of fame. It was a reminder to use every chance you get to tell your sons and daughters how proud you are of them, whatever their achievement.

It was hard for our children to believe that when Ed and I graduated high school, there were no family members there. Our dad was on a merchant ship someplace, and our mother had hurt her back and was unable to travel. It would have been an eight-hour trip for our aunts and uncles, and the farming season was in high gear. We knew they were all proud of us. We never thought much about not having a family member present.

After a son, daughter, three granddaughters, and two great-granddaughters, maybe I understand my own parents a little better. We want better for our children than we had for ourselves.

Our son spent most of his early years in Blackshear with my parents after their retirement from the Merchant Marines and the Slash Pine Community Action. Gary spent time with them on camping, fishing, boating, and bird hunting. They did things my parents never had the resources or time to do with us or we did with our own children.

Dr. R. Grady Snowden Sr., pastor of Arlington Baptist Church, said maybe the Lord should have let us be grandparents first and then parents second.

Financial Advice

Not long ago, I was talking with a young married couple and asked how married life was treating them. All was well, they said, except for their parents, who were "trying to run our business, and tell us what to do with our money—what to buy and what not to buy."

I asked if they minded me asking a personal question. They agreed.

"Have you borrowed money from your parents?" I asked.

They responded, "Yes."

My advice: "Do not borrow money from your parents unless you are willing to hear their advice on how to spend the money. They are not likely to loan you their hard-earned money without attaching financial advice with it."

As you already know, there are exceptions to most cases. If you have more than one adult child, there may come a time when one may have a greater need for money than the other. Often it's the one who likes to sleep late and has a problem finding or keeping the "perfect" job.

If there is a true need for money, give it to them with no expectation of receiving it back. Consider it a gift rather than a loan. And to be fair with the other children, let it be known that one day it will be deducted from their inheritance.

Even married children do keep score. The exception, of course, is when one child has a physical or mental need that requires more guidance and support.

If you do not feel you can or you are not willing to make an outright gift, then take them to the bank. Hopefully the banker will make a loan to the adult son or daughter.

Remember, if you cosign for the loan, you might find that the outright gift was a better idea.

❖

Mules

Memphis, Tennessee, is best known as the home of Elvis Presley. It is also the home of the blues and two great business success stories: Holiday Inn and FedEx.

Recently, two of my pilot friends, former Navy Captain Alan Ware and Commander David Loy, were visiting in Rome. Currently, they are pilots for FedEx. David recently bought a Mooney aircraft and was in town to pick it up.

A few months ago, Carolyn and I went with a church group to Branson, Missouri, and on our trip home we stopped in Memphis for a day to tour Graceland and look at Elvis's airplanes.

Few people know, however, that Memphis at one time was the mule capital of the world. When Carolyn and I were flying from Jackson, Tennessee, to Clarksdale, Mississippi, to visit with our friends Gene and Sandra Carver, we flew over the rich crop land known as the Delta in northern Mississippi. The big tractors were plowing in formation like a flyover of B-29s. I thought that must have been a sight to see when the plowing was done with mules. Today, all the mules are gone, and many of the tractors have been replaced with big gambling casinos on the mighty Mississippi.

In South Georgia my granddaddy on my mother's side of the family, Joe Peacock, was quite an entrepreneur for his time. He bought eleven one-horse farms. A one-horse farm was usually 100 acres—enough for a tenant farmer to feed his family.

Tenant farmers, or sharecroppers, furnished the labor while the landowner furnished the soil and seed to grow crops. Most of the time, the sharecropper owned his own mule, which was like a member of the family.

I never understood why it was called a horse farm rather than a mule farm. Usually horses were used for transportation or sporting events. Mules did the farming.

Some people may get nostalgic about those times. However, there is not much excitement anymore at actually looking at the south end of a northbound mule.

I mention Berry College a lot in this book. The active campus is 300 acres with the balance of 27,000 acres in pasture and woodland. Much of the money to buy the land was given by Henry Ford in the 1920s, and the great gothic buildings on campus are known as the Ford Buildings.

The business manager of the college, Mr. Gordon Kowen, called J. L. Todd and told him Mr. Ford would replace the school's mules with tractors if the mules were gone by Friday. Mr. Todd had a sharp mind for business, so he bought the last thirteen mules, gave them a bath, and sold them in Atlanta the next week for a ten-dollar profit on each mule. Mr. Todd went on to own and operate one of the largest and most successful auction companies in the country. It's fairly obvious that if you can see a profit in thirteen mules, the multimillion dollar land and building deals look a little easier.

In 2008 Berry College established an entire department to teach students how to write a business plan, accept assets, and make the assets grow and become profitable. This action plan is putting into practice what is being taught in the master of business administration degree program. I suspect the history of the mules teaches what a humble beginning can become.

Mules have two famous characteristics: stubborn and hard-working. They are now part of our history.

Something new and improved often comes along. Remember the foolishness of the man who ran the patent office saying that about everything that could be invented had already been invented? Ha! Even Forrest Gump thought his former lieutenant invested their shrimp boat money well—in a good fruit—Apple.

Courage and Fear

I taught instrument flying to Dr. Larry McSwain when he was president of Shorter University in Rome. Speaking at our church recently, he mentioned my name in his sermon, which caused me to sit up and listen a little better.

He talked about Esther's courage in the Bible. I often wished I were more courageous. Ed and I were fairly good fighters—mostly with each other. Our dad was a boxer in the Army, and he trained some pretty good fighters, namely J. D. and Travis Davis.

Travis always wanted us to spar with him with a promise that he would not hit us very hard. Don't ever believe that a boxer won't hit hard.

When I was about thirteen, I wrote for the Charles Atlas Course. They kept my quarter and never sent me the course. They promise you would have a strong body, never be picked on at school, and the girls could not keep their eyes off you.

Some surveys have indicated the three greatest fears are of flying, snakes, and public speaking. I sat up a little straighter when I received that important information.

I have been on the speaking circuit for many years. I still get butterflies sometimes when standing before a crowd. Currently, I am president of Tillman Aviation University, teaching people to fly. Ed and I used to catch snakes on our farm, but I still respect them.

My big dream was to walk down the street like Crocodile Dundee and not be afraid of a group of hoods. I don't carry a gun or a big knife, but I do have a good pair of non-skid running shoes.

Now, back to Dr. McSwain's message: Have the courage to do what is right.

I am still scared of shots, and the people at the blood bank told me not to come back. I was bad for their business, and they did not have time to keep putting cold, wet towels on my forehead.

Our fears are different. But when it comes to doing what is right, we should all have courage.

Ways to Waycross

In my early childhood (1933–1950) our family farm was about the same distance from the South Georgia towns of Alma, Blackshear, and Waycross. This was in the days prior to TV. After Sunday lunch the men would sit on the front porch or the woodpile and discuss the weather and how the animals and crops were doing.

Sometimes there was heavy discussion about what was better, Ford or Chevrolet. One of my uncles would poke fun at another for driving a Plymouth. In those days we had never heard of Honda, Toyota, and Mitsubishi.

One Sunday afternoon, there was heavy discussion over the best way to go to Waycross from the "Forks," properly named because our church, school, and community was between two creeks: Big Hurricane and Little Hurricane.

One uncle said the roads were better to go through Blackshear to Waycross. Another said to take US 1. Another said to go through the flat woods. My grandfather, Walter Tillman, spoke up and said, "By gosh, boys, there are lots of ways to Waycross."

Walter married beautiful seventeen-year-old Nicey Johnson, and they raised four girls and three boys on a fifty-acre farm. My dad was the oldest. My grandmother, Nicey, lived to be nearly 100.

In my business and professional career when a committee or team meeting seemed to get heated about the best way to complete a project or task, I often said, "There are lots of ways to Waycross."

Yes, in most families, companies, civic, or church groups there is more than one viable way to do something. There are lots of ways to Waycross.

In my first book I talked about management style. Companies, associations, clubs, and churches are often seeking the same goal but with different management styles.

I have seen managers, company presidents, and organizational leaders build people. They take great pride in seeing their people grow and mature as the organization grows and accomplishes its goal. Each person is encouraged to be himself or herself.

Conversely, I have seen a company go broke and break the spirit of most of its employees due to dictatorial leadership and greed or an unwillingness to let people be themselves and to accept that there is often more than one way to do something well.

After college and my time in the U.S. Army, I was employed in 1957 with Independent Life in Jacksonville as a door-to-door insurance salesman. You have to have a high tolerance for pain for this kind of work. You learn great lessons, like when someone says she does not have any money, it means she does not have money for you.

That lesson served me well after marriage. When I tell Carolyn I do not have any money, it means "none." When Carolyn says no money, she means none for me. The few dollars she has in the top chest of drawers is some she is saving for something special.

Independent Life moved us from Jacksonville to Chattanooga, and then to Jackson, Tennessee. Then we were moved to Indianapolis. On our own we moved to Lexington, Kentucky, before joining the management team with State Mutual Insurance in Rome in 1974.

Someone gave us some sound advice a long time ago: "Keep your children in a good neighborhood, a good school, and a good church, and you will do well."

At that time I did not realize how important that advice was. When you suffer a great loss and people show up, call on the phone, and write letters from all over the country, you realize you received some good advice by the people who touched your life.

Honda, Toyota, Mitsubishi

A few years back, President Gloria Shatto invited me to be the guest speaker at Founder's Day at Berry College. This was a big ego boost to go back and present words of wisdom to students, friends, and classmates.

You might remember that my brother and I both flunked algebra and English at Blackshear High School. What is even more surprising to me, after retiring as vice president of State Mutual Insurance Company, I worked for Berry College as assistant to then-president Scott Colley. That does not say much for higher education. My assignment was mostly to help raise money and to fly the president and other staff people. I was not diagramming a sentence or working any algebra problems.

After my Founder's Day presentation Dr. Roscoe Perritt, a Berry College graduate, said, "Why don't you come to Shantou University (in China) and speak to our students and professors?"

"On what subject?" I asked.

"Insurance and banking and how it works in America," he said.

Having spent forty-five years in insurance and receiving the CLU (Chartered Life Underwriters) designation from the American College in Bryn Mawr, Pennsylvania, I knew a little about insurance and figured I could fake the banking part.

I told Roscoe I would be in Hong Kong in three months and could go from there to Singapore. It seems that in many countries outside the United States, someone knows someone who will help you through the system. Roscoe went back to China and started making arrangements. I had a contact in Hong Kong who would prepare the visa to get me in and out of China.

Carolyn and I were traveling with two other couples from Georgia. She would tour Hong Kong with them for a few days, and I would rejoin them for a company meeting in Singapore.

Several people gave me advice. Mostly, they said to find someone who speaks some English and stay close to them. At the Hong Kong airport I met a young Asian gentleman who spoke some English. I thought, "I have my leader."

I told him I was going to speak and conduct a seminar at Shantu University in China. He got excited and said, "I am a Korean doctor and studying acupuncture at Shantu University."

This was the first time in my life I looked around the very large Chinese airline and felt both special and a minority. I had the only gray hair on the plane, and I was the only one who was not Asian. By this time my new Korean doctor friend said my Georgia accent did not sound like people he met from New York.

By this time we were laughing and trying to understand each other. He mentioned that I talked much slower than his New York friend. I asked him if he knew why Georgia couples had large families. Soon we were laughing together, and I realized how humor crosses international boundaries.

The plane landed at the Shantu airport, and I knew Roscoe would be waiting there. What I did not know was that the security people put my Korean friend in another line and marched his group quickly through the airport.

Once again, I was alone, listening for a few words of English. I saw three very distinguished Asian men talking. Somehow, I just know the Lord takes care of people.

The three men spoke just a few words that sounded good to me. I asked them, "Do you speak English?"

"Yes," they said. "Do you speak Japanese?"

I said, "Yes," and immediately added, "Honda, Toyota, Mitsubishi." They slapped their legs with laughter, and I knew a little humor had saved me. They walked me through the security process, and just outside was Roscoe waiting with a group from the university.

The first evening at dinner, I sat next to the university president, an appointee of the Chinese government. He spoke no English but delighted himself and other guests in showing me how to use chopsticks. After some time he presented me with a fork with great laughter.

The next night, hundreds of students came to the seminar. I asked Kim, a student from the economics department, why so many students would come to my presentation. She said, "Oh, you very important American come to our university. Make us very proud."

Just before my ego popped some of the buttons off my shirt, Kim added, "We come hear you speak, we get half-day off school." We enjoyed a laugh, and I knew once again that humor is a great bond.

None of the professors or students had visited America. I drew a large outline of the United States and pointed to Rome in Northwest Georgia. The students were aware of two locations: Disneyland in California and Disney World in Florida. It seems Mickey Mouse is famous all over the world.

The students had a good understanding of property insurance, but did not seem to understand the human life value of life insurance.

❖

Sister Jo

Josephine (Jo) was two years older than Ed and me. Our Grandmother Peacock called her "Phine." She was five feet, eleven inches tall. A beautiful young lady, Jo married Jim Winters, a chemist from Tennessee. They had three beautiful daughters.

Jo was a graduate of Blackshear High School and Massey Business College. She helped Ed and me during our school years and helped us pay for our first car. She was an avid NASCAR fan.

She and Jim lived in Jacksonville for their first ten years of marriage and then Atlanta for the next thirty-five years. Ed had been the grand marshal at Darlington and always had a ticket to the Daytona 500. Every Sunday night, Ed and Jo would talk after the Sunday NASCAR race.

Jeff Gordon was her favorite driver for a long time. I think she finally put him aside and started pulling for Jimmie Johnson. She always liked Bill Elliott, Dale Earnhardt, A.J. Foyt, Rusty Wallace, and the one who did back flips after winning a race.

She lived about a year after Ed died. I don't know exactly how things are in heaven, but if it's anything like we were taught in Sunday school, Gary and Hannah are enjoying their Uncle Ed and Aunt Jo.

Laugh Yourself All the Way to the Bank

Some people say not to talk about religion, politics, or money. Now, if you are looking for happiness by earning lots of money, just forget it. However, I have had no money and money. I can assure you, money is better.

I heard a good sermon recently on Mark 8:36—"What does it profit you if you gain the whole world and lose your own soul?" Most people

I know who have made lots of money tell us it's not the destination but the journey. Being rich and having money are relative terms. The more money you have, the more relatives you have.

We are told if you are on welfare and live in America, you are richer than ninety percent of the world population. I hope this book will have the average person laugh a lot and have all the money you need.

Recently, I read about people who have won millions playing the lottery and are broke within five years. And it's really sad to read about the professional athletes and successful entertainers who earned millions and then spent or lost it all.

Money is about choices and priorities. If your family earns $50,000, $75,000, or $100,000 each year, you just need to decide what is important to you. Maybe choose a bass boat instead of a cabin cruiser. Avoid credit card by paying the balance to zero each month. Perhaps consider a good used truck or car next time. Make wise choices about education to avoid being part of the student loan crisis so many face now.

The Two-Percent Rule

One of my uncles was a successful farmer. He said he only wanted two percent. He bought a pig for one dollar and sold it for two. He bought a cow for $100 and sold it for $200. He bought some land for $1,000 an acre and sold it for $2,000 an acre.

"Just two percent," he said.

I'm not sure about the math, but he smiled and even laughed all the way to the bank.

It does not matter what you do vocationally as long as you love what you do and you are making an honest living.

Ed and I loved to read the comic section of the newspaper—what we called the "funny paper." It was always good for a laugh. We especially liked Frank and Ernest, Blondie, Snuffy Smith, and Born Loser.

I still like to laugh. We were in California and went to Dr. Phil's show. He did a great job in helping people with some real problems, but there wasn't much laughter. On the other hand Steve Harvey had two families competing for money, yet everyone was laughing.

Laughter is good even when dealing with serious matters like money—whether we're trying to win a little more on a game show or applying the "two-percent rule" to farming.

Humor Mixed with Good Advice

Accept that some days you're the pigeon and some days you're the statue. Always keep your words soft and sweet just in case you have to eat them.

Always read stuff that will make you look good if you die in the middle of it. If you can't be kind, at least have the decency to be vague.

If you lend someone twenty dollars and never see that person again, it was probably worth it. It may be that your sole purpose in life is simply to serve as a warning to others.

Never buy a car you can't push. Never put both feet in your mouth at the same time because then you won't have a leg to stand on.

Nobody cares if you can't dance well. Just get up and dance.

Since it's the early worm that gets eaten by the bird, sleep late. The second mouse gets the cheese.

When everything's coming your way, you're in the wrong lane. Birthdays are good for you; the more you have, the longer you live.

You may be only one person in the world, but you may also be the world to one person. Some mistakes are too much fun to make only once.

We could learn a lot from crayons. Some are sharp, some are pretty, and some are dull. Some have weird names, and all are different colors, but they all have to live in the same box.

A truly happy person is one who can enjoy the scenery on a detour.

A Personal and Hopeful Word

Maybe you will think of your family as I share about mine. Remember that sometimes a hug, a smile or shared laughter is what helps us get through another hour, day, week, month, or even year.

The cell phone rang, and Carolyn told me Gary's plane was down.

"I'll be home in twelve minutes," I replied.

Gary, Hannah, and two of her girlfriends lifted off from the Rome airport for a pre-Christmas holiday trip on December 17, 2005. The planned trip would take them to Craig Field in Jacksonville and down the coast of Florida to an island in the Bahamas.

The girls, all juniors in high school, were so excited about the trip. They played volleyball together and were part of a Bible study group.

Denise and Gary have two other daughters, Rachel and Bonnie Grace, who followed in their sister's footsteps by playing on the volley-ball team at Darlington School in Rome. In December 2005 Denise, Rachel, and Bonnie Grace decided to stay home to get ready for Christmas activities. Hannah and her friends were to be gone for just a few days.

Since that time Rachel attended LSU and married Jon Peaden. They have two daughters, Ella and Emma. Bonnie Grace graduated from Samford University and is now working in Washington, DC.

Denise married Harry Rowland. Tamara married Jeff Smathers.

Hannah was the first grandchild on Gary's side of the family and on Denise's side of the family. She did not lack for attention.

She loved books, and her granddaddy, Boyce Dooley, a Georgia Tech graduate, had her doing math problems early on. I just guessed what the numbers stood for since Ed and I were so good at algebra that we took the same subject two years straight.

When she was young, I used to ask Hannah questions: "How do you like school?" "Who is your teacher?" "Who are some of your friends?" "What is your favorite subject?" Regardless of her answers, we were a proud Granddaddy and Grandmother.

One time, Hannah announced that she had never made but one B in school. "Hannah, we are so proud of you," I said. "Your Uncle Ed and I never made but one B as well." Her young mind did not get the humor in my response, but her Grandmother Carolyn knew the truth had been told.

On Saturday morning, December 17, 2005, I was giving a Civil Air Patrol friend a flight lesson about the same time Gary and the girls were to depart Rome in his Cessna 195. We planned to follow them to the Rome VOR (Variable Omni Range, a navigation aid for pilots), eleven miles south of town, then rock our wings and bid them good wishes for their trip.

I asked Gary about his flight plan. They would fly just west of Atlanta and then Victor-243 to Craig Field in Jacksonville. Carolyn and I lived in Jacksonville the first nine years of our marriage, so we were familiar with their route of flight, which I had flown many times.

Both Gary and Tamara were born in St. Luke Hospital in Jacksonville. I had earned a pilot license in an Army flying club managed by the renowned editor of *Flying* magazine, Richard Collins. He was my flight instructor and best man in our wedding.

After college Gary owned and operated Gary Tillman Insurance Agency and Aviation Insurance Brokers of North America. Denise joined Gary in the business after some time as an auditor with Georgia Kraft and with her dad in the cable TV business.

Denise majored in accounting at Berry College in Rome. Gary graduated from West Rome High School, lettered in track and cross country at the University of Georgia, and later graduated from Cumberland University. After college Gary returned to Rome and coached the Berry College girls track and cross country teams.

Gary said he would stop in Ft. Pierce or Ft. Lauderdale to clear customs and get the required Coast Guard life jackets. I had bought four Coast Guard-approved life jackets and suggested he might like to take them.

It seemed after age sixty-five that I liked to do a lot of things I had not done or could not afford as our family was growing. My friend Howard Alexander suggested I Sea-Doo and join him, Doyle Buffington, and Charles Green every Wednesday afternoon at Lake Weiss. I was hoping sometime Hannah, Rachel, and Bonnie Grace would also enjoy the Sea-Doo.

Gary took the life jackets I had bought for boating purposes along with other safety equipment for his trip.

Anna Kipp, Hannah's classmate and the daughter of an airline captain, and Rachel Hostetler, a champion swimmer at Rome High School, were aboard. Gary would be pilot in command, and Hannah was his acting copilot. We had given her a logbook, and I was looking forward to helping Gary teach her to fly. She would be going away to college in a year and a half, and her travel would increase.

The weather was not good after they landed at Craig Field in Jacksonville, so Gary decided they would spend the night in Jacksonville. The next day, Gary and the girls arrived at Craig Field mid-morning on December 18, 2005.

He filed a flight plan to South Florida where he would land and clear customs. He had flown this trip many times and knew the lay of the land. The coastline is like one long runway from Jacksonville to Miami.

As time passed, I reflected on the fact that his first flight, at six weeks old, was in a Cessna 172 and his last flight would be from Craig Field in a Cessna 195. All the legal information is recorded by the Federal Aviation Agency, and his last several minutes are recorded.

Gary had earned a private and commercial license with an instrument rating in single- and multi-engine aircraft. He was also working on his instructor's rating.

The next morning, after takeoff from Craig Field in Jacksonville, approach/center cleared him to 6,000 feet. The clouds covered Jacksonville, but he would soon be in the sunshine looking down on the coastline and much of Florida by the time he arrived over Daytona.

As he approached 6,000 feet near St. Augustine, he was off the coastline and was cleared. Then something went wrong. We don't know what. Some say carb ice; some say water in the fuel. According to the legal people, he handled the emergency as he had been taught. He had asked for vectors to the beach. The controller thought best to try to put him on the Instrument Landing System, which kept him over water rather than the coastline.

The accident has been studied and reviewed by the best legal and aviation industry minds in the world. Gary's last transmission was, "We are going to 'ditch' (a term used for landing in the water). Please send help."

Anna was recovered but did not live. She had on her life jacket. Rachel, a champion swimmer, survived. I'm not sure if she was in the water an hour and forty-five minutes or forty-five minutes. She was taken to the hospital, and her parents drove from Rome to get her. She finished high school and went on to college.

The St. Johns County Sheriff Department, other law enforcement in adjoining counties, the U.S. Navy Search and Rescue, Florida State dive team, and others searched for Gary and Hannah for sixteen days.

Major Chuck West and Sheriff David Shores of St. Johns County said they would not give up until they were found.

Ms. Miller, our family advocate with the sheriff's department, served our family in a wonderful way with hourly and daily reports as needed. Television and radio reporters, newspaper writers, and other media were kind to us and reported in a professional way as the search progressed.

Darlington School, where Hannah and Anna attended, had lost other high school students off the west coast of Florida in a boating accident just months earlier. Our community had lost some of its finest young people. This is true with all schools that suffer a loss of their young people.

Gary and Hannah were found by shrimp boat operators on Monday, January 2, 2006, and their memorial service was held on Saturday, January 7, 2006. It just happened that our chief of police, Hubert Smith, was on vacation in St. Augustine at the time of the accident. As we walked the dock each day and waited, he was with us.

Delos and Dee Yancey made arrangements for food for out-of-town friends and family. Delos and Joanne Yancey gave us the key to their condo. Dee made arrangements to fly Rachel and her family to St. Augustine to help in the recovery. Dee had Tamara picked up in Atlanta when she returned from the Middle East for a quick trip to St. Augustine.

Denise, Bonnie Grace, and Rachel returned to Rome to attend Anna's service. Dee and Delos Yancey, Andy and Edmond Cash, and Mike White provided us all aircraft to get to St. Augustine as quickly as possible.

The pilots, Wallace Reese and Bob Parker, would not accept payment for their service. They are our pilot friends. Frank Barron was at his place at the beach. Dr. Paul Ferguson from Rome was at the beach for New Year's 2006. They both checked on us each day.

Each time I see a news report of someone losing a child or of a family member who is missing, I just hope they have a network of friends and family to support them.

Howard and Gail Alexander had our house ready for our return in sixteen days. Gary and Denise lived across town from us. In Rome that's about twenty minutes and much less if you make all the lights.

Denise was getting the same support. Also, her mother and daddy lived thirty miles north of us in Trion. They were receiving the same kind of personal kindness. David, Denise's brother from Warner Robins, Georgia, and Gary both had planes and often would take Gary and Denise and Gail and Boyce Dooley on vacation.

Hannah thought Uncle David was the best. Like her Papa Dooley, he knew how to help her with math, also being a Georgia Tech graduate.

While we waited sixteen days in Florida, Chief Hubert Smith was making arrangements with Mayor Ronnie Wallace and City Manager John Bennett for the same kind of police escort given to a fallen officer. Gary had served on several city boards and made an excellent contribution to the advancement of our city. Ronnie was one of Gary's running buddies and was invited to do the eulogy for him.

In honor of Hannah, the Darlington High School choir sang. Ann Hook, one of Denise's best friends who was also close to Hannah, gave the eulogy for Hannah.

I'm not sure we should judge a funeral by the size, but I guess it says something of the life you lived. Someone once said, "Don't be too impressed with yourself. You can judge the size of your funeral by the weather that day."

Yet Aunt Bert said, "I have not seen a funeral like this since John Kennedy Jr."

More than 2,000 people filled the sanctuary of Rome's First Baptist Church. Dee Yancey flew ten officers from the St. Johns County Sheriff

Department with Sheriff David Shores and Ms. Miller, our family advocate, to Rome for the service.

We had not named any pallbearers, but as our pastor, Dr. Joel Snider, got out of his car, the uniformed officers stepped forward to carry the bodies to their final resting place. Denise said, "They are not here, but in heaven." That helped us bear the final moment of the graveside service.

As Dr. Snider spoke his last words to our family, the flying team from the Rome airport made a low flyover with a little rock of their wings to both Gary and Hannah as to say, "Well done, my good and faithful ones."

Absence from the body, presence with the Lord.

A New Beginning

As Ed and I drove a few miles from his home during the last months of his life to watch the waves roll in at Jacksonville Beach, he would often say, "As surely as the waves come in, they will come again." Then he would usually add, "As surely as the tide goes out, it will come again."

During our talks in North Georgia, living in the foothills of the Blue Ridge Mountains, we were reminded that for every valley there is a mountaintop. Ed would say, "You know that would 'preach,' and for every mountaintop there is a valley." Living in both has its rewards.

Since losing Gary and Hannah, I have heard words of intended comfort such as, "This earth's loss is heaven's gain" or "The last breath on this earth is the first breath in heaven." I want to believe, and I do believe; we have to keep doing the best we can.

I did not realize even in our town how many people had lost children and grandchildren. Even though you are hurting inside, you have just got to keep on smiling, remembering the good times you had together.

It is not just the pain of death we experience and endure. Many families lose to divorce, poor health, or the loss of a job or business they spent a lifetime to build. Some have lost savings due to poor economic conditions or a job that didn't pan out. The list goes on.

Yet we must hold our heads high and keep on smiling. Our coach used to say, "You win some, you lose some, and some are rained out." Indeed, tomorrow is a new day.

For those who suffer loss, may you receive the comfort you need. May the tide roll back in your life and the mountaintops remind you to keep looking up. I hope you have a strong faith and believe that life's greatest reward is to help someone else along the way.

Whenever possible, share a special chuckle with friends or family, and never repress laughter.

CPSIA information can be obtained
at www.ICGtesting.com
Printed in the USA
FFHW012100131118
49387793-53704FF